3-31-95

Jan,

It takes a courageous person to pursue their dreams real estate, but it takes a "great" person to help others be courageous. I know you will enjoy this book.

Ed

JOE GANDOLFO, PhD
DONALD JAY KORN

SELL & GROW RICH

THE **10** HABITS OF HIGHLY SUCCESSFUL SALESPEOPLE

Dearborn
Financial Publishing, Inc.

Publisher: Kathleen A. Welton
Associate Editor: Karen A. Christensen
Senior Project Editor: Jack L. Kiburz
Interior Design: Lucy Jenkins
Cover Design: David Corona Design

© 1993 by Joe M. Gandolfo, PhD, and Donald Jay Korn
Published by Dearborn Financial Publishing, Inc.

Printed in the United States of America.

93 94 95 10 9 8 7 6 5 4 3 2

Library of Congress Cataloging-in-Publication Data

Gandolfo, Joe, 1936—
    Sell and grow rich : the 10 habits of highly successful
salespeople / Joe Gandolfo, Donald Jay Korn.
      p. cm.
    Includes index.
    ISBN 0-79310-512-9
    1. Selling. 2. Selling—Psychological aspects. 3. Selling—Case
studies. I. Korn, Donald Jay. II. Title.
HF5438.25.G363 1993   93-3611
658.8'5—dc20   CIP

DEDICATION

I dedicate this book to all past salespeople and future salespeople, who are the backbone of our world economy.

▼

Foreword

**A GHOST GETS HIS CHANCE: A FEW WORDS
FROM DONALD JAY KORN**

This is a salesman's book, written for salespeople, but it's not *just* a book for salespeople. No matter what you do, you sell, so you should know how to do it right.

The image of a salesman hasn't changed much over the years. Up in the morning, good-bye to the family, briefcase in hand, into the car and off on a round of sales calls. Waiting rooms, presentations and, on a good day, signatures on the dotted line. About the only difference in this popular perception is that the "salesman" is just as likely to be a saleswoman in the 1990s.

Well, there still are salespeople like that. Lots of them. But there are also many salespeople out there who don't fit the traditional mold. For example, doctors. Every appointment with a patient is a sales call. A doctor needs to "sell" the patient on taking medicine, changing diet or whatever treatment is called for. If the patient doesn't buy, the treatment won't work. Moreover, the doctor must sell each patient on coming back for the next office visit, rather than changing to another doctor. The same is true with lawyers, who must sell clients on the value of their advice. Some lawyers must sell judges and juries, too.

What about the prototypical middle-aged Middle American, a middle manager with a mid-sized company? Even if you never see or talk with a customer or spend your whole career in data processing or accounts payable, you still have to sell. You have to sell your ideas to your colleagues, and you have to sell yourself to your supervisor if you're interested in raises or promotions. And in today's unsettled corporate world, you never know when you'll have to sell yourself to a prospective new employer.

So everybody sells. More precisely, everybody should know how to sell. To learn how, you need a good teacher. That's the purpose of our book: to reveal the secrets of one of the world's sales legends, Joe Gandolfo. It's truly a book for everyone, but especially a book for anyone with a career in sales.

MODUS OPERANDI

As you'll learn, Joe has had an incredible career, one that has now spanned five decades—the 1950s, 1960s, 1970s, 1980s and 1990s. He holds just about all the sales records there are, in and out of life insurance.

Best of all, Joe is a teacher as well as a salesman. He has the ability to explain the sales techniques that have worked for him, to explain them in such a way that all salespeople, novices or veterans, can apply them to their own careers. Beyond techniques, Joe shows you how to bring out the best in yourself, no matter what your talents and abilities.

Before starting, I'd like to explain how we organized this book. As you'll see, it's mainly written in the first person, the "I say" point of view. After this short preface, the "I" becomes Joe's voice. This is his story, which I helped to organize.

However, we break from first person in Part Four, "Conversations with Joe Gandolfo," for a few chapters in dialogue. These chapters spell out Joe's selling strategies in some detail, so we thought you should read them in Joe's own spoken words.

Before getting into sales methods, we spend a few chapters on the fundamentals. As Joe insists, you need to get your spiritual, familial, physical and mental houses in order before you can sell and grow rich.

After our conversations on sales techniques, we cover some topics, such as presentations and closings, in some detail. Then we close the book with chapters on selling in the 1990s, from seminar selling and women in sales to technology and taxes. Altogether, we think you'll come away with everything you need to succeed as a salesperson—and a great deal more.

A SATISFIED CUSTOMER

When I said everyone sells, I meant everyone. Even free-lance financial writers. Since I've begun working with Joe, I pay a lot more attention to what the editor is saying—and less to what I'm saying—when I propose article ideas. I look into people's eyes when I talk; I watch their mouths while I listen. In a tough economy, my business has been pretty good. Maybe it's just a coincidence. Maybe it's not.

Read our book. Take Joe's fundamentals to heart and work on his techniques. You'll be sold on yourself, which is the step you must take before you can sell anyone else.

DONALD JAY KORN

Contents

▼
Preface

Born in the hills of Kentucky more than 50 years ago, I lost both parents early in my life. If a person of Sicilian heritage, growing up in Kentucky and orphaned as a teenager, can make it to the top, so can you.

Whenever I read a book or magazine, I take what I think will help me or my clients. I never criticize the author. Whenever I listen to someone, I remember what I think will fit me or my clients. I never criticize the speaker.

I've been selling ever since the 1950s. I have over 10,000 clients in all 50 states, from billionaires to blue-collar workers, people from every walk of life, every color and creed.

I found early in my life that people don't care how much you know until they know how much you care. If they find something wrong with what you're selling, that means they've found something wrong with you. Ideas are a dime a dozen, but the people who put them into practice are priceless.

The theme of this book is, *Selling is 98 percent understanding human beings, 2 percent product knowledge.* On the following pages, I will prove it to you. As Oliver Wendell Holmes said, "Many times ideas grow better when transplanted into another mind, than in the one where they sprang up."

God has given each of you talent: That's God's gift to you. What you do with that talent is your gift back to God. I hope this book will help you to sell and grow rich, not only in material wealth but in the kind of wealth that will make you a greater human being, the wealth that will help you to serve others. Make this your priority, after your belief in God, and the rest will take care of itself.

Put God first, give Him His share and you will sell and grow rich.

JOE M. GANDOLFO, PHD

▼

Acknowledgments

I would like to thank my wife, Carol, and my three children, Michael, Diane and Donna. They were very patient in those earlier years when I was working 19 hours a day, 7 days a week.

Next, I would also like to thank Don Korn, who took my ideas and put them down in a readable fashion. We've become very close, and we have both grown as human beings.

I would also like to thank my editor, Kathy Welton, who initiated the idea for this book. She has been wonderful to work with.

Finally, I would like to thank my invaluable administrative assistant, Kim Bauer, for all of her extra hours in helping to put this book together.

Above all, I would like to thank God, who has given me the talents that I possess.

▼

Introduction

"Just because He doesn't answer doesn't mean He doesn't care; some of God's greatest gifts are unanswered prayers."

FAITH FINISHES FIRST

You can sell. I don't have to meet you personally, I don't have to know anything about your strengths and weaknesses, to know you can sell and grow rich. If you truly want it, you can have a successful career in sales. All you need is faith: in God, in your family, in your own ability. Then you need the determination to carry through.

There's one other characteristic you must have—a feeling for other people. *If someone finds something wrong with what you're selling, it means he or she has found something wrong with you.* People don't care how much you know until they know how much you care.

You'll never convince anyone to buy anything because it's good for you, the seller. The buyer wants what's good for him or her, the buyer. If you understand human nature, you'll figure out what your customers want and offer it to them. That's great selling. That's how I sell, and those are the secrets we're going to reveal in this book.

▼▼▼

If someone finds something wrong with what you're selling, it means he or she has found something wrong with you.

THE JOE GANDOLFO STORY

As you'll learn in chapter 23, I begin every sales call by telling the prospect something about myself. This is a technique I use so a client will trust me and, eventually, buy from me. Because I want you to trust me—to "buy" my sales secrets and put them to work for you—I'm going to start out our book the same way, by telling you something about myself.

I have little sympathy for anyone who says he or she didn't succeed because they "didn't get the breaks." Few people go through life from one pinnacle to the next, effortlessly scaling peak after peak. More often, the winners are those who climb back up after a shattering fall.

That's certainly been my experience. I went through an incredibly frustrating adolescence that was "unfair," as society's apologists would put it today. But I didn't let the knockdown knock me out. Instead, I dusted myself off and got back into the batter's box, more determined than ever to realize my goals.

Here's what happened: My parents came over from Palermo, Sicily, the "old country." After an arranged marriage, they grew to love each other deeply. Settling down in Richmond, Kentucky, about 25 miles east of Lexington, my father worked long and hard. He started as a truck driver and became the largest produce broker in the state as well as the owner of the local Packard auto dealership.

I was born in 1936 and grew up with an older sister and two younger brothers. In those Depression and World War II years, my childhood was comfortable but not affluent; all four children slept in one bed until my sister got old enough to rate her own. Then, when I was 11, my mom became ill. For two years, I watched her body waste away, consumed by cancer, until she died on Mother's Day, at age 39.

My dad decided the best place for me was a military school, so off I went to Kentucky Military Institute, coping as best I could with my new surroundings. While I was there, my dad died of a heart attack, leaving all of us orphans.

One of my uncles declined an appointment as guardian. He basically said, "The heck with those kids." He took whatever my father had left and left us with virtually nothing. We became separated, and I never saw my sister or my brothers again.

▼▼▼

People don't care how much you know until they know how much you care.

LONELY TEENAGER

Life was even lonelier after my father's death. There were no birthdays, no Christmas celebrations. I cried myself to sleep every night.

So how did I survive? My belief in God carried me through. I decided to turn my life over to Him. Once I could unconditionally accept God's will, I could live with my loneliness.

In my unhappiness, I focused on sports. Ever since I was a small child, I had wanted to play baseball, so that's what I did at military school, in addition to quarterbacking the football team. Besides playing on the military school's baseball team, I was on a championship American Legion team. I was good enough, in fact, to get some professional offers after I finished high school.

Instead, I went to college on athletic scholarships. First to Vanderbilt University and then to Miami University in Ohio, where I continued to play baseball. At Miami, I majored in math. I also made the best sale of my life: I convinced a beautiful blonde coed named Carol Lorentz to drop her fiancé and marry me. The first time I asked her out, I had my shirt off, in biology class, so the professor could draw a heart for a demonstration. She turned me down then and for three months after that, but I finally convinced her to go out with me. Persistence, like patience, can be a virtue.

A DEAL I COULDN'T REFUSE

After college and a brief minor-league baseball career, I was teaching math and coaching at a high school in Fort Lauderdale, Florida. A local life insurance agent named Jim Burns asked me if I wanted to be in the insurance business. At that time, I was married, with two kids, making $213 a month. Jim told me I could make $450 a month, so I went into insurance. I remembered what my father had told me before his death: "Be independent. Be your own boss."

Back then, in the late 1950s, I didn't get a lot of sophisticated sales training. The insurance company sent me to Baton Rouge, Louisiana, and gave me a rate book and said, "Go get 'em, tiger." I rented a room in a private home for $35 a month and began selling. (Carol and the kids were with her parents in Ohio.)

Well, plenty of doors slammed in my face, and many phones slammed in my ears. Still, I worked 19 hours a day, 7 days a week, and it paid off. In my first week, I wrote $92,000 in contracts. Within six months, I had broken all the company's records, making $18,000 in commissions, so I thought, "Maybe this is for me."

I'm disturbed by laws designed to prohibit winners from being winners in order to prevent losers from being losers.

LITTLE POND, NO FROGS

Carol and the kids joined me after this initial success, and we rented an apartment. However, we didn't like the cold, wet winters in Baton Rouge so we moved to Lakeland, Florida, a college town with a sunnier climate. Best of all, Lakeland had no Chartered Life Underwriters and no members of the Million Dollar Round Table, the industry's honor roll. I figured the lack of competition would help me get started, and I was right. Today, even though I have policyholders throughout the United States, Lakeland is still my home base.

How did I start out in Lakeland? Selling to ministers. I knew they would give me appointments, even if everyone else in town turned me down. Besides, I thought ministers weren't being called upon by other insurance agents, who probably didn't feel comfortable discussing religion. Not only did I sell the ministers, but I got the names of young newlyweds or couples preparing for marriage. These couples, in turn, trusted me because I was referred by their ministers.

Then I started calling on funeral homes, another market neglected by other life insurance agents in town. Most of the local funeral homes employed young interns studying to be embalmers or funeral directors, so they were good long-term prospects. What's more, they were familiar with the subject of death, so I found that I could sell them fairly easily.

I went to every drugstore and called on the pharmacists there. I went to librarians. I went to professors at Florida Southern, the local university. The more people I called on, the more sales I closed.

By my sixth year in the business, at age 29, I qualified for the Million Dollar Round Table, the industry's highest award. Since then, I've made it every year. I was the first salesman in history to sell over $1 billion of life insurance in a single year. I've been called "one of the ten greatest salespersons in the United States" and "the Number One insurance agent in the world."

PLAYING TO WIN

I've stayed with sports, too. I'm a ranked tennis player and a brown belt in tae kwon do (a form of Korean karate), the only person ever to go from a white directly to a green belt, skipping the yellow belt. Whatever I do, I play to win. Therefore, I take care of myself—I don't drink or smoke. I'm a vegetarian, having given up meat at age 34, although I occasionally eat fish.

When you compete hard all the time, on the court and on the job, you learn to admire other winners and disdain those who never got in the game. I'm disturbed by laws designed to prohibit winners from being winners in order to prevent losers from being losers. You don't need some kind of a preference to succeed: Government cannot give anything that it first doesn't take away from someone else. If you're a winner, you'll win, no matter how far back in the race you start out.

Government cannot give anything that it first doesn't take away from someone else.

PART ONE

Build a Solid Foundation

Our objective on earth is holiness,
not happiness.

1

▼

When the Heaviest Hitter
Is on Your Side

"Aim at heaven and you will get the earth thrown in. Aim at earth and you will get neither."

C.S. LEWIS

"Every happening, great and small, is a parable whereby God speaks to us, and the art of life is to get the message."

MALCOLM MUGGERIDGE

You may wonder why I am starting a book about selling with a chapter on religion. The answer is simple: You need to have certain fundamentals in place before you succeed in anything, in any profession or career. First of all, you need to be right with the Man Upstairs. No matter how you earn a living, God has to come first. You can't separate your personal life from your business life. *Our objective on earth is holiness, not happiness.*

In every field of endeavor, nobody has a perfectly easy time. The winners are those who overcome adversity. That's especially true with selling. You need strength to deal with all the rejections, all the prospects who say no. If you can't get the strength you need from your husband, your wife or from someone else, you have to get it from another source: the Man Upstairs.

NO SUBSTITUTIONS

To call upon this inner strength, your behavior must be based on the Ten Commandments. Remember that they're called "commandments"—*God commanded; He didn't make suggestions.* God gave you the lead; now you have to follow.

Following those commandments will definitely help you in your career, if you commit to them enthusiastically. Enthusiasm really means "God within." If you're enthusiastic about what you do and the way you do it, you'll be successful.

On the other hand, you can't succeed without having God within. If you're not right with the Man Upstairs, you won't be a success, no matter what field you're in. All the great human beings have placed God first. Every giant I've ever met, in any field, believes in that one fundamental—you need to be right with the Man Upstairs. Sports stars such as Orel Hershiser, Michael Jordan and Herschel Walker thank God for their ability.

God commanded; He didn't make suggestions.

SINCERITY SELLS

Salespeople especially need spiritual strength. No matter what you're selling, you have to sell yourself first. Without sincerity and inner peace, you cannot be a great salesperson.

Every prospect goes through mental gymnastics before buying something. They say to themselves, "If this salesperson seems right with God, I'll trust him to not lie, cheat or steal from me. Therefore, I think I will go ahead because I know he has my best interest in mind." If you don't believe that, you're living a fantasy life.

Suppose you're not right with God and the prospect detects that. That's when you hear prospects say "I want to shop around." They're really saying "I don't trust you." That's why you lose sales. It doesn't have anything to do with product knowledge.

People buy trust. If you're not right with God, you can't tell the truth. People can tell you're not right with God when they look at you and you look away—they won't trust you. And you won't sell anything.

Therefore, a salesperson who is at peace with himself or herself makes a good impression on prospects. People in other walks of life need religion, too. Take athletes, for example. The mark of a great athlete is the ability to concentrate. You can't concentrate if your mind is not right, if you're not right with the Man Upstairs.

THE RIGHT STUFF

I feel that I'm right with the Man Upstairs because I've always relied on Him for help with my career. When I started in this business, I was living in Baton Rouge, Louisiana. I can't tell you how many hours I spent in the Catholic chapel at Louisiana State University, praying to God with tears in my eyes and wondering if I was doing the right thing. I'd ask myself if this was what I wanted to do for the rest of my life. I thought about hanging it up, but that would have been the easy way out. God gave me the strength to stay the course.

Faith carried me through, and I'm not the only one. After all that Rose Kennedy has been through, she was asked how she had managed to cope. She said she thought about Christ and the Virgin Mary. As she put it, "Put God first, give God His share of your earnings, then sit back and enjoy the adventure."

If you don't pray to God, God can't answer your prayers.

So what can salespeople learn from Rose Kennedy and Joe Gandolfo? Be devout. Go to your place of worship regularly, whether it's a church or a synagogue or a mosque. And you should tithe. Give God His share. Many of this nation's greatest business success stories, men such as J.C. Penney, H.J. Heinz and William Colgate, were faithful churchgoers who tithed.

You may think that tithing has gone out of style, but that's not the case. I know one auto dealer who had the worst Chrysler dealership in the United States, so he went over to Pontiac and promised to give half his income to God. Since then, he has netted millions of dollars each year. *If you don't pray to God, God can't answer your prayers.*

A lot of people think that they have been so bad that God will never listen to their prayers. That's a bunch of nonsense. I don't care what a person has done; if that person gets down on his or her knees and asks for forgiveness, God will forgive and forget. He erases everything and you start over on a new slate. If you slip, you go backwards; but if you make an effort, you'll stay in God's good graces. Once you become disciplined in your life and attempt this, the world becomes a better place.

PRACTICE WHAT YOU PREACH

God does not give us blessings because we deserve them or as a reward. Instead, the only reason He blesses us is so we can give to the needy. God's gift to every person is a certain amount of talent. And what that person does with this talent is a gift back to God.

Naturally, there's more to being devout than praying and tithing. Sometimes God's greatest gifts are unanswered prayers. You have to meet challenges on your own. Ask God's blessing on your work, but don't ask Him to do it for you.

To earn God's blessing, I try to follow the Ten Commandments. You need to practice your religion, not just preach it. A lot of people pray and can't understand why God does not answer their prayers. God doesn't answer prayers from those who don't obey His commandments. You can sit and pray all day long about finances, relationships and so forth, but if you are mean to your spouse or your kids, if you have a bad attitude toward people or if you are vengeful, you might as well be talking to a wall. God won't answer your prayers unless you get down on your knees and ask God for forgiveness for all the sins you've committed and try to live a good life within His commandments.

▼▼▼

Pray for what you need, not what you want.

DO UNTO OTHERS . . .

You should read your Bible seven days a week. Take a few minutes each morning, even if you have to get up a few minutes earlier. I even have a chapel in my office to help discipline myself. When Jesus Christ came on earth, He came to serve people, not to be served. We all need to have this attitude. If we all decided to help and serve other people, this would be a better world and we would accomplish our goals.

I'm a Christian, so I know that my task is to serve, not to be served. Help others before you help yourself. In fact, that's really the key to selling. You find out what will really help your customers and your clients, and then you sell it to them.

A good salesman not only tries to put himself in his customer's shoes, but he can love his customers if he believes in God. Everyone I look at, black or white or whatever, was made by God. I know God doesn't make trash. I can follow my faith and love my fellow humans.

SIN'S WAGES

Many people think they can get by on earth by lying, cheating, stealing, hurting other people, being arrogant or indulging in sexual satisfaction; but God will get their attention through disease, death or financial destruction. If you disobey God, you'll run into disaster, financial and otherwise.

Just look around. Drug dealers meet with violent deaths. People who indulge in excesses often suffer terrible diseases. Greedy people, for whom money, money and more money is their only goal, have financial disasters. People who lie, cheat and steal wind up with what they deserve.

All around us, you can see the consequences stemming from a lack of religion. There are more suicides now than ever before. There are also more divorces and kids going off the deep end. A lot of that results from a lack of fundamentals—from not having a base to fall back on in tough times.

▼▼▼

When adversity comes into
your life, God is shouting
to you. When peace and
pleasant things come into
your life, God is
whispering to you.

MAKE TIME FOR GOD

I have people coming to me all the time saying that they're having trouble selling. I ask if they practice their religion, and they say they don't have the time. Well, how can you pay attention to your work when something is cluttering your mind? You can't be so busy that you don't have time to listen to God. And if you don't listen to God, you'll have a harder time selling.

If something is bothering you, if you're not right with God, you can't concentrate on what you're doing. If you can't concentrate, you can't do any job well, especially in sales. When something is worrying you, you can't be productive.

Worry is a devil in people. If you think you have problems, you should go to a hospital or a funeral home once a day. Then you'll see what problems really are.

Even devout people worry, but they have an advantage. If you're devout, you can give your worries to God when you go to bed. Just say to God, "You're up all night anyway." You can let God do your worrying for you. I do that because I'm at peace with God. I'm no saint—I'm subject to the same temptations as anyone else—but I keep the proper perspective and stay disciplined. He comes first, and I never forget it.

ACCEPT THE INEVITABLE

I have a sign outside my office that says: "Everybody wants to go to heaven, but nobody wants to die." I think about death. I know I'll wind up six feet deep. But that's a very healthy, realistic attitude. I don't kid myself.

We should not feel bad about death because God loans us our parents, our spouses, our children and all the other people put on earth. God made them, and God has a right to take them away, so we should not be disappointed when people die. God loaned us His children for a certain period of time, and then that's it.

The talents you possess are God's gift to you—what you do with those talents is your gift back to God.

FAIR SHARE

To observe my religion, I do more than go to mass every morning. I give 50 percent of my adjusted gross income to God, and I give anonymously. No matter how much I give, I always get back twice as much. Once I gave $5,000 to charity. That same week, I got a check for nearly $11,000 from an oil investment I had made years ago and forgotten about. I do the best I can and trust in God to do the rest.

I always say, "Lord, I'll give you all the credit, and I'll take all the commissions."

SUMMING UP

- Everyone, including salespeople, must be comfortable with God if they want to succeed in worldly endeavors.
- As a salesperson, if you are right with God, customers will trust you; otherwise, your customers won't trust you, and you won't sell anything.
- To be at peace with the Man Upstairs, you should practice your religion and give to those less fortunate.
- Going to religious services and giving away money won't help unless you also follow the moral tenets of your religion.

▼▼▼

If you have fear of the
Lord and walk in His
ways, then you will enjoy
the fruits of your labor.
You will prosper and
be happy.
—Psalms 128:1–2

2

▼

The Home Team Advantage

"The family is the first essential cell of human society."

POPE JOHN XXIII

"The Presidency is temporary, but the family is permanent."

YVONNE DE GAULLE

"Without a family, man, alone in the world, trembles with the cold."

ANDRE MAUROIS

If having a good relationship with the Man Upstairs is the first fundamental for success in selling—or in anything else, for that matter—the second fundamental is a strong family life. When things are going smoothly at home, you can concentrate better on your career. My wife Carol may not know much about my industry, but she's helped me sell a lot of life insurance. She handles all the details at home, which frees me to take care of business.

When I started out selling life insurance, I'd get up at 2:00 A.M. and come home at 10:00 P.M., totally exhausted. Carol has said she'll put this on my grave marker: "While others slept, he was awake."

I didn't require Carol to get up and fix me breakfast or wait to have dinner with me. Her job was to take care of our house and our kids. I never let her forget that I needed her, loved her and couldn't do it without her. We've always worked together, as a team, and money is the way we keep score.

PAYING YOUR DUES

In those early days of my career, we had only one car in the family. I was working almost 17 hours a day, 7 days a week, so Carol would have the car for only 2 hours every Saturday, when she could do the laundry and the shopping. The only things we owned in our first seven years of marriage were a playpen and a high chair. Carol paid a dear price. But, as she said, "I made up my mind, when I first married Joe, I was going to have to share him with the rest of the world."

▼▼▼

The beginning of wisdom is the fear of the Lord. Understanding is avoiding evil. When you pray, pray for wisdom and understanding.

If you intend to sell successfully, don't kid yourself—you'll have to pay the price, too. I've seen more young salesmen (with a lot more talent than I possess) ruined because their wives say, "I want you to leave at 8:00 A.M. and come home at 5:00 P.M." So the guy gives up the chance for business success and dies inside. Too many women work so hard trying to make good husbands that they seldom make good wives. Such women can ruin marriages. Some people think that's one reason the divorce rate is so high.

After I had become well known for selling life insurance, a young man came to see me and said that he wanted to double his "production"—the amount of insurance he was selling. Here's how the conversation went:

J.G.: Tell me about your schedule.
Young salesman: I get up at 6:30 or 7:00 A.M., eat breakfast with my wife and kids and take them to school. I get in to my office about 8:45. . . .

▼▼▼

The greatest gift a father can give to his children is to love their mother.

J.G.: We don't need to talk any more. You're wasting half your life. You don't sell your wife and kids at breakfast; you don't get paid to take them to school. But if that's what you want to do, and you're happy doing that, that's fine. Just don't tell me you want to double production. It takes sacrifice. Unfortunately, it also means sacrificing time with your family.

PROMINENT TARGETS

I can hear you saying that your kids must be on dope, you're probably on the borderline of divorce and so on. That's not true. There are bound to be rumors about people who work hard and succeed. Others will say "See what work has done to that guy; it's killing him." As Stefan Edberg, Swedish tennis star, said after winning the 1992 U.S. Open, "When you are No. 1, you are on top of the world. It's like being on top of a mountain, and the wind blows hardest there."

In many cases, what the critics are really saying is, "I'm too chicken. I don't have the guts to go out and do what he does." If you say "I want to spent more time with my family," it's often a cop-out. You may just be too lazy to succeed.

FAMILIARITY BREEDS DISCONTENT

Contrary to popular myth, when you're a success, you don't always wind up divorced, with your kids on drugs. Just because you're not having breakfast and dinner with your family every night, there's no reason you can't be a good husband and father. When my children were young, I took the family out on Friday nights, "dated" my wife on Saturdays and put aside Sunday as a family day. As my daughter Diane says, "Dad spent excellent time with us, including some great trips and vacations, so we're very close now. I'm close to Mom, too, who's patient, really opposite of Dad. I can talk with them."

It's the quality of life you spend with your wife and kids, not the quantity of life. I'm not embarrassed to hug and kiss my kids, even my son. When I traveled, I called my kids every night. I told them that I loved them, and it was always great to hear them say that they loved me. The same is true with my wife. I need to tell her that I love her and hear her say that she loves me. *The greatest gift a father can give to his children is to love their mother (and vice versa).*

Surveys show that salespeople have fewer divorces than anyone else. The people getting divorced are those who work from 8:00 to 5:00—they see too much of each other.

DO AS I DO

When you're out in the world working those long hours, you're providing an invaluable example for your kids. My son Michael once said, "We saw that you achieved your goals through sacrifice and discipline." As Robert Frost said, "Americans are like a rich father who wishes he knew how to give his sons the hardships that made him rich."

If you don't work hard, you're deceiving yourself. Your spouse and your children won't respect you. Many kids today go off on the wrong track because they don't see how hard parents must work to succeed. My children learned from Carol and me that if they work hard, they succeed. The same lesson can apply to your children. When they see that Daddy gets up early and goes to bed late, they see the results. *They learn through example that there are no shortcuts: that's the most valuable lesson your children can learn.*

When my kids were in school, they discovered that if they studied hard during the week, they'd make As. If they worked hard on the tennis court, they'd win tournaments. If they didn't work hard, they couldn't expect to win. As it turned out, my three kids were All-American tennis players and straight-A students.

I didn't spoil my children. They're not named after my wife or me, and they weren't expected to follow in my footsteps. I told them that I didn't care if they smoked, drank or committed crimes. That's their life, and I won't blame myself.

▼▼▼

They learn through example that there are no shortcuts. That's the most valuable lesson your children can learn.

Nonetheless, I'm proud of the way they turned out. Mike, who took a turn on the pro tennis tour, buys and sells phone companies. He worked for IBM for awhile and then went into business for himself. My daughter Donna is with AT&T leasing, and Diane is a leading Allstate insurance agent. As for Carol, who's a grandmother now, she does volunteer work and is a ranked tennis player.

My definition of success is to achieve the goals you set for yourself, not the goals someone else sets. Each person has a different appetite for success. My battery and motor happen to be revved up, and I have a woman who likes that about me. Without her, I never could have succeeded.

HELP WANTED

Things are different today than they were when I started out, back in the 1950s. Many salesmen, especially the younger ones, are married to women with their own careers. These men don't have the advantage I've always had; Carol took care of all the details on the home front so I'd be free to concentrate on selling.

Nevertheless, you *can* sell successfully even if your wife has a career. The trick is to hire someone else to do all of the housework—the cleaning, shopping, cooking, child care, etc. You probably can find quality help at reasonable rates by hiring teenagers, the elderly and the disabled.

Any expense is a consideration, especially when you're starting out, but the time you save is that much more time you can devote to selling. If your income from additional sales doesn't far exceed the extra cost of hiring help, you probably should consider another career.

SUMMING UP

- After God, the most important thing a salesperson needs is support from a spouse.
- Ideally, your spouse will handle all the child care and housework, freeing you to concentrate on selling.
- If your spouse works, too, it will pay for you to hire someone else to take care of business and personal chores.
- Just because you put in long hours at your job, your marriage and your kids aren't necessarily doomed. Spend quality time with your family members, and be sure they know that you love them.
- The best lesson you can give to your kids is to show by example that success comes from hard work.

3

▼

Taking Care of
Number One

"Good health and good sense are two of life's greatest blessings."

PUBLIUS SYRUS

"Ill-health, of body or of mind, is defeat. Health alone is victory. Let all men, if they can manage it, contrive to be healthy!"

THOMAS CARLYLE

"People often say that this or that person has not yet found himself. But the self is not something that one finds. It is something that one creates."

THOMAS SZASZ

"We have to learn to be our own best friends because we fall too easily into the trap of being our worst enemies."

RODERICK THORP

Besides God and family, every salesperson needs another crucial ingredient for success: good health. No matter how sincerely you pray or how loving your marriage, you can't sell while you're sick. You have to take care of yourself. Good health is everyone's major source of wealth. Without it, happiness is almost impossible.

Therefore, I toil as hard on my health as on my business. I work out for an hour and a half each day, and I maintain a strict vegetarian diet. My weight is 160 pounds—not a lot for someone who is six feet tall. When I travel around the country to speak, I get more compliments on my body than on anything else.

How do I manage to work out so much while maintaining my career? I get up at four o'clock in the morning so I can go to mass and communion and still have enough time to accomplish everything. In fact, successful people get up early. Anyone who sleeps more than seven or eight hours a night is sick. If you say there's no time for keeping in shape, that's a cop-out. *God gave you 24 hours a day. If you don't utilize them to the best of your ability, you deceive God, your family and yourself.*

Success begins when one acquires the habit of work.

WASTE MANAGEMENT

Another problem I avoid is overeating. Most Americans are gluttons—80 percent are obese. If God gave me two wishes, it would be not to have to eat or sleep. I hate to eat, hate to sleep—they waste time. Too many people waste their time sleeping and eating.

MASS MURDERERS

Of course, you should avoid smoking and excessive drinking. Every year in the United States, approximately 2 million people die. Out of the 2 million, 1 million deaths are classified as "premature" or "preventable." Furthermore, out of that 1 million, 500,000 deaths are due to smoking and 100,000 to excess drinking, according to Elizabeth Whalen, president of the American Council of Science and Health.

So don't smoke and don't drink too much if you want to be around to enjoy your success.

THE SPORTING LIFE

Physical conditioning should start early in life. Sportsmanship and competition stimulate a youth's ambition. *It's better and easier to build fit children than to mend broken adults.*

I've always considered myself a jock. I played football in high school and baseball in high school and college and even played minor league baseball afterwards. I played handball when I was younger and took up tennis when I was 34.

To stay in shape today, I have three main activities. I play a lot of tennis, competing in about 25 tournaments throughout the year. I practice tae kwon do, a school of martial arts. In addition, I use a form of stretching called tai-chi ch'uan. As we get older, we all lose suppleness, which you can replace with tai-chi. I also do 150 push-ups and 200 sit-ups every day. And I lift weights every other day.

Without being physically active, you can't be mentally active. Physical activity helps you work out your frustrations. When I don't work out, I'm a bear as a husband and father. As long as I'm exercising, I can keep up a demanding work pace and never get tired.

When I'm on the road, I always stay on eastern time. It keeps my body functioning normally. If I have to go to sleep at 7:00 P.M. and wake up at 2:00 A.M., that's what I do. I learned this trick from an airline pilot back in 1959, and that's what I've been doing ever since.

The price of leadership is loneliness.

CONFIDENCE BUILDER

The better you feel, the more confidence you'll have in your physical ability, and the better you'll perform.

If you don't maintain your body, you won't have the stamina you'll need to pursue success. There was a young sailor who was in the navy on a particularly rough cruise, when everyone was throwing up.

Captain: What's the matter, son? Have you got a weak stomach?
Sailor: No, sir, I'm throwing as far as the rest of them.

IT'S THE ONLY THING

No matter what your career, you have to compete to succeed. The better your physical condition is, the better you can compete. As the late Vince Lombardi, former coach of the Green Bay Packers, said: "It's a reality of life that men are competitive, and the most competitive games draw competitive men. That's why they're there, to compete and to win. They know the rules and the objectives of the game. The objective is to win: fairly, squarely, decently, but to win.

"In truth, I've never known a man worth his salt who, deep down inside, didn't appreciate the grind and the discipline. There's something in good men that yearns for and needs discipline and the harsh reality of head-to-head combat. I don't say these things because I believe in the brute nature of man, or that man must be brutalized to be combative. I believe in God and I believe in human decency. But above all, I believe that any man's finest hour is that moment when he knows he's worked his heart out in a good cause, and lies exhausted on the field of battle, victorious."

FROM PAIN TO GAIN

On the tennis court or in selling, my secret for being the best is simple. *Success begins when one acquires the habit of work.* Few people really know how to work to the best of their ability. As Abraham Lincoln said, "Work is so rare a merit it should be encouraged."

I've always been willing to work harder than anyone else to get what I wanted. Most people aren't willing to pay the price. Instead, most people are mediocre in their goals.

▾▼▾

A thoroughbred is
someone, a person as well
as a horse, who gives
every pump of his or her
heart to every second
of life.

MARATHON MAN AND WOMAN

Grete Waitz certainly didn't have mediocre goals when she arrived in New York in 1978 to run the New York City Marathon. She had been a championship long-distance runner in Norway, but when race organizer Fred Lebow asked her about her longest run, she said she had never run more than 12 miles. A far cry from the 26-mile-plus marathon.

"I had pain in my side," she recalled, thinking of the race. "I was coughing. I was just hurting." When she reached the finish line, she threw her running shoes at her husband and said she would never run another marathon. That was until she found out she had set a world record for women, just over 2 hours and 30 minutes. She went on to win the New York City Marathon 8 other times, winning 14 of the 16 marathons she entered in her career.

In the meantime, Lebow, who ran 68 marathons in his own career, was struck by brain cancer in 1990. He put on weight and lost hair. The doctors gave him six months to live, but he got up from his hospital bed and began walking and then running. He figured out that 67 laps around the roof of the hospital made one mile, so he began running laps. By 1992 he was out of the hospital and running 20 miles at a time.

Anyone who sleeps more than seven or eight hours a night is sick.

In November 1992, on the day of the New York City Marathon, retired marathoners Grete Waitz and Fred Lebow ran the course together.

SOMETHING HAS TO GIVE

The price of leadership is loneliness. Winners have few real friends. I don't have people over to my house to visit; I don't visit other people; I don't belong to any civic organizations or country clubs. I don't like it, so I don't do it. It's not necessary for success.

NO LOOSE ENDS

Every day I pay every bill, return every call and answer every letter. My head doesn't hit the pillow until it's all done. If you do that, you're telling people that they're important. If you don't return calls or letters, you're saying to people, "I don't care about you."

When you call a doctor or lawyer, aren't you happy when someone gets on the line and says "How can I help you?" Well, it's the same for people who call you. They want help with a problem, and they want help right away. They want peace of mind. So call people back.

READ THEM OR WEEP

God said that you should work six days a week and rest one day. Humans invented vacations and retirement. Americans think too much about their vacations and retirement and not enough about their work. That's why we're losing ground to the Japanese and the Germans.

Now that I'm older and successful, I don't put in the 100-hour workweeks any more, but I still have a demanding schedule. I stop working at six or seven o'clock, and I work every day except Sunday.

I use the extra time for studying, three to four hours each day of the week. Most people vegetate; they don't read enough. I read *The Wall Street Journal*, *USA Today*, local newspapers and magazines such as *Forbes*, as well as my trade magazines. If you don't keep up with what's going on in the world, you'll fall behind your well-informed competitors.

THE WINNING TICKET

You shouldn't make silly excuses for not succeeding. If you think you're short on time, don't do everyday chores. You can hire people, including retirees, the handicapped and young kids, to do the routine things while you focus on your career.

As a native of Kentucky, I know that thoroughbreds win races. *A thoroughbred is someone, a person as well as a horse, who gives every pump of his or her heart to every second of life.*

▾▼▾

God gave you 24 hours a day. If you don't utilize them to the best of your ability, you deceive God, your family and yourself.

SUMMING UP

- You need to take care of yourself to be successful in your career.
- Work out regularly, eat moderately and get enough—but not too much—sleep every night. Don't drink too much or smoke at all.
- If you're in good condition, you'll be able to work hard, which is a must for a successful career.
- Besides taking care of your body, you need to stay in shape intellectually. Devote time each day to reading so you can keep up with your profession and with what's going on in the world.

▾▼▾

Anyone can succeed by
working for half a day, five
days a week. You have to
decide which half: the first
12 hours or the second
12 hours.

4

Attitude Beats Aptitude

"Industry is a better horse to ride than genius."

WALTER LIPPMANN

"To achieve, you need thought. You have to know what you are doing and that's real power."

AYN RAND

You don't have to be good-looking to be a salesperson. You don't need to be a genius, an athlete or a spellbinding speaker. You don't even need a formal education.

What you need is to have your fundamentals in place. Fundamentals mean more today than they did when I was starting out. You need to be right with God, your spouse and your body. In addition, you need a positive mental attitude.

If God gave me two wishes, it would be not to have to eat or sleep.

The most influential book I've ever read is *Think and Grow Rich*, by Napoleon Hill. This book changed my life. On my desk in my office are words I live by, and they are taken directly from that book: "Anything the mind can conceive and believe, it can achieve."

Although the book was written more than 60 years ago, it still rings true today. Hill interviewed more than 500 great people of his time, including Andrew Carnegie and Thomas Edison. He asked them, "Why does one man fail to achieve his goals in life while another succeeds?" He got different answers, but the underlying message was the same: Success comes to those who think positively.

Hill was working on a book targeted at black Americans when he died. After a period of time, the Napoleon Hill Foundation turned the incomplete manuscript over to author Dennis Kimbro, who wrote *Think and Grow Rich: A Black Choice*. He naturally included the stories of leaders from the black community, so it serves as an excellent source of inspiration for minority salespeople.

For example, Alonzo Herndon was a slave for the first seven years of his life, until the Civil War ended. He worked at a number of tasks, from field hand to peanut seller, before he found his niche—as a barber. He moved to Atlanta in the early 1880s and worked his way up to the ownership of an opulent haircutting establishment with marble floors and crystal chandeliers. This was the only black-owned shop on Atlanta's main business street.

Herndon made even more money in real estate, eventually becoming the owner of a prime business block. Then he saw yet another opportunity: life insurance. Blacks had an extremely difficult time buying life insurance then, so Herndon started a company that insured them. Agents included young black college graduates who couldn't work for white companies. Started in a one-room office in 1905, the company had 70,000 policyholders by 1911. Today Atlanta Life Insurance Company has over $135 million in assets.

HELPFUL HINTS

Other books I particularly like are *Life's Not Fair but God Is Good*, by Robert Schuller; *The Wonderful Spirit-Filled Life*, by Charles Stanley; and *Magic Power of Your Mind*, by Walter Germain. All of these books, sermons and so forth are nothing more than the first two fundamentals. If you're right with the Man Upstairs and have a great spouse at home to take care of all the details, you're free to dedicate yourself to your vocation. That's how fundamental life is: God, family and yourself.

Anything the mind can conceive and believe, it can achieve.

SWEET DREAMS

The other key ingredients for success are the ability to dream, tenacity and a willingness to work hard. *If you dream, day and night, something happens to your body that helps you attain your dreams.*

When I was a little boy, I was given a baseball mitt by Earl Combs, a Kentucky neighbor who starred on the great Yankee teams of the 1920s. After that, I slept with my mitt every night of my youth. I dreamed that I'd field a ground ball in the major leagues. That dream eventually came true.

Early in my career, when I went to an industry meeting, I didn't like not being known. Now, I'm the featured speaker at those meetings.

Almost every year I attain one of my dreams. I wanted a son for my first child, a left-handed athlete. I wanted gorgeous blonde and brunette daughters. Well, I got them. Don't be afraid to dream big dreams. If you'll be satisfied batting .250 or getting to the quarterfinals, that's where you'll wind up. If making $25,000 a year is your dream, you won't earn more. Dream of being the best you can be.

If you're a young salesperson, maybe you're a little frightened and intimidated by the top producers. Well, they're not ten feet tall. They're usually no bigger or better looking than you are. You can do what they've done as long as you have the same ambitions, the same dreams.

And while you dream of your own success, don't stop your children from dreaming, too. Show them how to dream and how to step into those dreams.

▼▼▼

If you dream, day and night, something happens to your body that helps you attain your dreams.

LION-HEARTED

Dreaming works for you, no matter what your chosen profession. Take Chris Spielman, the son of a high-school football coach. He grew up three blocks from the Pro Football Hall of Fame, and he never wanted to do anything but play pro football. He went to the Hall of Fame so often that the guards eventually let him in for free.

When he was five, he surprised his grandmother by tackling her. When he was nine, he'd stuff hot dogs in his back pocket so the family dog would chase him around the backyard, so Chris could work on his agility.

He wound up a two-time All-American at Ohio State, only the second linebacker ever to win the Lombardi Award as the nation's outstanding lineman. Spielman is someone else who knows the value of getting up early. At Ohio State, he'd get to the stadium film room at 6:00 A.M., beating head coach Earle Bruce.

But when Spielman graduated, there were doubts about his ability to realize his dream of playing pro football. The "experts" believed he was too short and slow for a pro linebacker. Despite his outstanding college record, Spielman wasn't even picked in the first round of the player draft.

That was a mistake for the teams who passed him up. Drafted by the Detroit Lions, Spielman continues to be the first player to work out each morning and the last to leave each night. One day another Lion volunteered to lift weights with Chris and his brother Rick, who was also trying out for the team. Midway through the workout, the exhausted non-Spielman ran to the bathroom and threw up.

"Are you all right?" Chris asked.

"Yeah, yeah."

"Well, hurry up. It's your set, and you're holding us up."

And what was the payoff for this dedication? Chris Spielman has been a starting inside linebacker from day one for the Lions. He set a team record for tackles as a rookie and led the team in tackles in each of his first four seasons, going to the Pro Bowl three times.

Why is Spielman so determined to be the best, to play a violent sport despite the pain? "It has to do with commitment," he says, "to yourself, to your teammates, to your coaches, to the people who are relying on you to play."

DREAM A LITTLE DREAM

Dreaming is a must for success, in sales or any other pursuit. The dreamers are the ones who sell the $10 million insurance policies and win tournaments on national television.

But you can't dream that you'll be a world beater one day and beat the world the next. As the saying goes, "The longest journey begins with a single step." You need to start somewhere and gradually build yourself up to being a champion. If you set small goals for yourself and achieve them, you'll go on to attain bigger and bigger goals and you will become a champion. Along the way, your self-confidence will increase, each time you reach one of your goals. You'll *know* you can succeed; you'll *expect* to succeed—out of habit—so you *will* succeed.

The longest journey begins with a single step.

When I first started out, my goal was to make at least one sale a day every day—even if that sale was only for a $5,000 or $10,000 policy. Each day I would come home knowing that I had closed a sale. Soon I knew that I could close sales. My self-confidence increased, and I expected to close a sale every day. The little successes eventually grew into large successes, and I began to sell six- and seven-figure policies.

I went through a similar process as a public speaker. When I was younger, the thought of standing in front of an audience and giving a speech made me sick to my stomach. So I started out speaking to small groups—maybe five or six agents in a local office. I told myself that it was just like speaking to some of my baseball teammates. There was nothing terrifying about it as long as I knew my subject thoroughly.

Over the years I began to speak to slightly larger groups, in training sessions. Then I'd speak at small meetings. I was eventually able to travel the world and speak to audiences numbering in the thousands, even the tens of thousands. I have been on national television many times, speaking to millions of people. Thanks to the self-confidence I've built up over the years, I'm always completely at ease.

So don't expect to sell and grow rich the very first day. Start with realistic goals. Tell yourself you'll make 20 cold calls every day, for example, and get at least five appointments out of those calls. Aim for one new client every day. If you get one new client every day, that's 250 a year. Keep those clients satisfied, grow with them and mine them for solid referrals. Before you know it, you'll have a client base in the thousands, and you'll be closing those big-ticket, high-commission sales you dreamed about.

SUMMING UP

- The remaining fundamental that's necessary for sales success is the power to think positively.
- If you dream big dreams, you'll push yourself until you attain those dreams.
- On the way to achieving your big dreams, set modest goals you can attain in a short time period.
- As you become accustomed to realizing small dreams, you'll build up your confidence to the point where you can fulfill big dreams.

5

▼

Persistence Pays Off

"I do not know anyone who has got to the top without hard work. That is the recipe."

MARGARET THATCHER

"A clay pot sitting in the sun will always be a clay pot. It has to go through the white heat of the furnace to become porcelain."

MILDRED WITTE STRUVEN

"The right moment for starting on your next job is not tomorrow or next week; it is 'instanter,' or in the American idiom, 'right now.'"

ARNOLD TOYNBEE

People frequently ask me this question: "Did you really sell billions of dollars' worth of life insurance, or are you stretching it a little?" I always respond, "The only thing that needs stretching is your mind." As Penn State football coach Joe Paterno says, "You don't know what you have until you have to use it."

Great salespeople need to be inventive, always looking for new solutions to a customer's problems. Alexander Graham Bell, who should be the salesperson's patron saint, wrote, "An inventor is a man who looks around upon the world and is not content with things as they are; he wants to improve whatever he sees; he wants to benefit the world; he is haunted by an idea; the spirit of invention possesses him, seeing materialization."

You don't know what you have until you have to use it.

CUSTOMERS COUNT

Successful salespeople must dream for two. Besides your own dreams, you have to understand what the customer wants. To succeed, any salesperson must put the customer first.

Approach customers the way you'd like to be approached. If you're cheerful and helpful, people will repay you in kind. As the saying goes, "Be tender with the young, compassionate with the aged, sympathetic with the striving and tolerant of the weak and the wrong. Sometime in life you will be all of these."

People who focus on helping others live longer. Nothing is more important in this world than helping human beings. I've changed my investment strategy to reflect this philosophy. I invest in companies that help other people. Wal-Mart, for example, gives customers a chance to buy a variety of good products at low prices. It's a helpful company. I don't buy shares in cigarette companies.

TRUE BELIEVER

My philosophy of helping others carries right through to my career selling life insurance. Someone once said, "If you want to be happy for a year, win the lottery; if you want to be happy for a lifetime, love what you do." Well, I'm in the lifetime category because I love what I do.

I've sold billions of dollars' worth of life insurance because I believe in my product. You can't sell something you don't believe in.

I never hesitate to say that I sell life insurance because I know that it really helps people. As Sue Laramore has written in *Decision* magazine, "On the 'me' days, and the 'I want' days, and the 'nobody notices me' days, I will remember that I like myself better on the 'let me be a help to others' days."

One of my first clients from my days in Baton Rouge died shortly after he bought a policy from me, leaving a pregnant wife. I thank God that I could provide protection to that family. Not only did I become a believer in life insurance; I became a customer. Now I carry millions of dollars of insurance on my own life.

If you want to be happy for a year, win the lottery; if you want to be happy for a lifetime, love what you do.

WORK ETHIC

Besides believing in your product, you need to believe in yourself. Then you need to put in long hours of hard work. Here are some of my favorite thoughts about achieving success:

- Too many people stop looking for work after they've found a job.
- The best job you can have is to go back and work at the job you're already at.
- Excellence is nothing more than tenacity of purpose.
- If you have no purpose in life, it doesn't matter how long you live.
- You don't know what you have until you have to use it.

As former pro football coach George Allen said, "Every single human being has a certain amount of talent. Unless you use that talent, to the best of your ability, 24 hours a day, every day of your life, you deceive your God, your family, but, above all, yourself. This is what life is all about."

All these sayings carry the same basic message: Sacrifice and discipline are necessary for success.

▾▼▾

Life is like a turtle. If you don't stick out your neck, you don't go anywhere.

ALIVE AND KICKING

George Allen also said that "a person without problems is dead." Everyone has problems, no matter how positive your mental attitude. Thinking positively won't make your problems disappear, but it will allow you to deal with them. As General Patton asserted, "Every man is made up of brains and guts. If you only have half, you're only half a man."

Joe Paterno is a football coach whose players have an outstanding record of succeeding in the classroom as well as on the field. Here's how he advises his players to deal with their problems:

- You must always do what you're afraid to do.
- You either get better or you get worse.
- The will to win is important, but the will to prepare is vital.
- To win, you must play as though you can't lose.

Paterno's advice is similar to that of John Wooden, the great former UCLA basketball coach:

- Peaks create valleys.
- Develop yourself; don't worry about opponents.
- There's no pillow as soft as a clear conscience.
- Why do so many people dread adversity when it is only through adversity that we grow stronger?
- The main ingredient of stardom is the rest of the team. As Paterno and Wooden would both agree, it's amazing how much can be accomplished if no one cares who gets the credit.

A STICK IN TIME . . .

Winners don't confuse motion with progress. You need to set goals and work toward them if you want to succeed.

Have you heard the story about the swallows at San Juan Capistrano? Every year they fly from Buenos Aires, Argentina, to this little town in southern California, arriving each year on March 19. Nobody knows how they do it. Not only that, but they fly 6,000 miles to get there, mainly over water. Now swallows can't swim. They can't fly 6,000 miles nonstop either. So how do they do it?

Each swallow carries a twig in its beak—that's a big burden for such a tiny bird. When the swallows get tired, they drop the twigs in the water, float on them and rest. Then they fly some more. Swallows know that they have to pay the price—that is, carry a heavy load—if they want to reach their goal. The same goes for people. You have to pay the price for success.

And don't equate financial success with success. What counts most is how you achieve your success.

STRESS-TESTED

Steel must go through fire before it can become a knife. Coal must undergo incredible pressure before becoming a diamond. You can't know true happiness until you've been miserable. If you're determined not to let obstacles stop you, you'll succeed, with or without natural gifts.

Life is tough, and then you die. While you're alive, though, you might as well play to win. As Adolph Rupp, legendary basketball coach at the University of Kentucky, said, "If winning is not the only thing, why keep score?"

Life is like a poker game. If you don't put anything in the pot, you won't get anything out.

SECRET HARVEST

As you go through this book, you might think that what I say won't relate to you. That's a foolish attitude. I'm a product of a lot of listening and reading. I take what will fit me and throw the rest away. That's what you should do as you read on, discovering my sales secrets. The great jurist Oliver Wendell Holmes once said, "Many times ideas grow better when transplanted into another mind, rather than the one where they sprang up." Every great idea is based on, built, adapted and changed from the ones that came before it. That's what it means to *stand on the shoulders of giants.* So you should take my advice and fit it to your own personality and your abilities.

God gave everyone two ends—one to think with and one to sit on. Heads you win; tails you lose.

SUMMING UP

- Great salespeople think about helping their customers rather than helping themselves.
- You need to believe in your own product or service.
- Once you have these beliefs in place, hard work can help you to sell and grow rich.

▼▼▼

To be great, you can't be concerned with what other people think of you.

▼▼▼

PART TWO

Smooth Selling

The more time you actually spend selling, the more sales you'll make.

6

▼

A Matter of Time

"That which is in disorder/Has neither rule nor rhyme."

FRANCIS CARLIN

"Pythagoras, when he was asked what time was, answered that it was the soul of the world."

PLUTARCH

"Does thou love life? Then do not squander time, for that is the stuff life is made of."

BENJAMIN FRANKLIN

Let's say you're in sales. You wake up in the morning, at peace with God and your family and healthy in body and mind. You say to yourself, "Now I'm ready to sell and grow rich."

But then what? You can't just walk out the door and close a million-dollar sale, no matter how strong your fundamentals. You have to go somewhere and sell your product or service to someone. In short, you need a plan.

For salespeople, the key to planning is time management. The more time you actually spend selling, the more sales you'll make. To make sure you spend as much time as possible, face-to-face with clients, you need to work smarter as well as harder.

Each business or industry has a prime selling time. That may be early in the morning, during the nine-to-five business day or in the evening after dinner. Once you've determined what your prime selling time is, arrange your schedule so that you spend most of that time actually selling.

Time is too precious to waste.

In my field, I have found that prospects are easiest to reach in the morning, before they start their own nine-to-five jobs. That's why I'm up at four o'clock each morning. I can go to church, do some reading and still be face-to-face with my clients at six or seven o'clock.

I can also be on the phone with my clients, voice-to-voice, at those hours. Once you have met a client and established a personal rapport, it's a lot more time-efficient to conduct subsequent business by phone, rather than chase around from appointment to appointment.

The times that you're not selling shouldn't be dead times. In the evenings, on the weekends or whenever you're not actively selling, you can take care of paperwork and all the other necessary details. In addition, you can read newspapers, magazines, product literature and so on—whatever you need to keep up with your work.

Do you spend a lot of time in your car? Don't listen to oldies-but-goodies on the radio. Instead, listen to cassettes. There are cassettes that condense books and articles or that teach you how to learn a language, etc. You can even buy a minicassette player with earphones so you can listen and learn while you're walking or jogging or riding in a cab.

As great men and women from Plutarch to Benjamin Franklin have known, time is too precious to waste.

ELUDING THE TIME TRAP

How can you arrange your time so that it's well spent? Begin by understanding some of the obstacles to efficient time management. In his classic book, *The Time Trap,* author R. Alec Mackenzie relates that a group of salespeople in one of the largest North American insurance companies named nearly the same time wasters as a group of black leaders of religious organizations. Those time wasters included the following:

- Attempting too much at once
- Lack of delegation
- Talking too much
- Lack of planning
- No priorities
- Inability to say no
- Procrastination

If you address these concerns, you'll improve your time management enormously.

I hire competent people and let them take a lot of the load off my shoulders.

"Attempting too much at once" and "no priorities" are two sides of the same coin. You have only a certain number of hours available for selling, so you must focus first on the most important activities and then on the next most important activities, and so on down the line.

"Lack of planning" is related to a lack of priorities. You can't just get into your car in the morning and start driving around looking for sales. You need some reason for going one place at 7:00 A.M. and another place at 8:00 A.M., etc.

How can you plan your time to pursue your priorities? Many years ago Charles Schwab (the president of Bethlehem Steel, not the discount broker) asked management consultant Ivy Lee this question: "How can I get more things done with my time?" Lee gave Schwab a piece of paper and said, "Write down the things you need to do tomorrow and rank them in order of importance. The first thing in the morning, start with Number One and keep working until it's completed. If your priorities haven't changed, go on to Number Two. And so on. Stick with each task, no matter how long it takes, as long as it's your top priority."

A few weeks later, Schwab sent Lee a check for $25,000, saying this was the most profitable lesson he had ever learned. Within five years,

Bethlehem Steel was the largest independent steel producer in the world, and Schwab was worth $100 million.

You can follow Lee's advice today. Each night before you go to sleep, make a list of the most important things you need to do the next day. Then, do them in order of importance. You'll wind up getting the important things done and skipping the nonessentials.

For salespeople, setting priorities may mean focusing on the largest potential sale, with a reasonable possibility of success. If you can sell a $1 million policy or a $100,000 policy, which sales call will you schedule first? You'll obviously choose the $1 million policy unless the chance of closing the sale is so remote that it's not worth your time. If, however, the $100,000 policy is a stepping-stone to the eventual sale of millions of dollars worth of policies, you'll choose to make that sales call first.

If you spend too much time telling prospects what they need to buy, you're not listening to them telling you what they want to buy.

MANY HANDS, LIGHTER WORK LOAD

The next time waster, "lack of delegation," is a particular concern of mine. Too many salespeople waste their time mowing the lawn, going to the bank, handling clerical work and so forth. You're much better off paying someone else 5, 10 or even 20 dollars an hour to do your busywork, freeing yourself for selling.

You can do this at home or work. Plenty of teenagers, retired people and handicapped people are willing and eager to come into your home to do routine chores for modest pay. If you judge carefully, you can find reliable helpers. I've been doing this for years.

I do the same thing in my office: I hire competent people and let them take a lot of the load off my shoulders. I have an experienced controller who not only handles my accounting and bookkeeping; he calculates the financial details used in my sales presentations. I have assistants who handle my speaking engagements, travel arrangements, speech preparation and materials shipments to customers; they're constantly on the phone following up on sales leads.

All the employees in my office have an insurance license so they can service existing clients. They share in any commissions they generate, in addition to their salaries. I might have kept some of those commissions for myself by dealing with those clients directly, but in the long run I wind up with higher total commissions and well-motivated employees.

I make it a point to hire not only highly qualified people but also methodical ones. Before I hire someone, I always inspect the inside of his or her car. If the car is messy, I won't hire the candidate. Someone who's not neat in his or her personal life will probably carry over those sloppy habits to the office, which I can't afford.

TALKING IS A WASTE OF TIME

Another time waster, "talking too much," is an obvious sales killer. *If you spend too much time telling prospects what they need to buy, you're not listening to them telling you what they want to buy.*

As for "inability to say no" and "procrastination," they're easy enough to deal with once you have a plan that spells out your priorities. You can say no to anything that doesn't fit in with your current top priorities; if you're working on your top priority, you're not procrastinating.

Once you're focused on the essentials, time management will fall into place.

SUMMING UP

- Time management is crucial for successful selling.
- One of your main objectives should be to spend as much time in direct selling and as little time in nonselling activities.
- When you're not selling, try to use the time productively.
- Delegating nonsales tasks to others can free more selling time for you.
- The key to time planning is to set priorities and pursue them.

7

▼

Be a Know-It-All

"Knowledge is power."

FRANCIS BACON

"Knowledge, in truth, is the great sun in the firmament. Life and power are scattered with all its beams."

DANIEL WEBSTER

Selling is 98 percent understanding human nature and 2 percent product knowledge. That's been my message throughout this book, and it's certainly the way I sell. But that doesn't mean that you can forget the 2 percent of selling that's product knowledge. The more you know about your product or service, the more you'll sell.

Product knowledge and human empathy are actually complementary. You can listen to your prospects telling you what they want to buy; if you have a store of product knowledge, you can make the appropriate recommendation, meeting their expressed needs, and close the sale.

Look at it another way. Suppose you're a stockbroker. Your prospect tells you that he or she wants safe, secure income in retirement. You hear the word "income," and you recommend the stock with the highest dividend on the New York Stock Exchange. However, this is an extremely risky stock as it pays a high dividend because the price is low in anticipation of a dividend cut. Sure enough, the dividend is cut, and your client winds up with no income. You have an unhappy client, no possibility of future sales and the very real possibility of a lawsuit. All because you didn't take the time to learn your business.

▼▼▼

Unless you know what you're doing, you're like the actor who goes on stage without knowing his or her lines or the surgeon who operates without going through internship and residency.

Unless you know what you're doing, you're like the actor who goes on stage without knowing his or her lines or the surgeon who operates without going through internship and residency. You're not a professional. As John W. Galbreath, one of America's leading real estate developers, has said, "You've got to know everything about your business. There's nothing more disrespectful or presumptuous than going into a man's office and not being able to answer his questions. If he asks a question related to your business and you reply, 'I don't know,' you've wasted his time. You've made a fool of yourself and insulted him."

HOME STUDY PROGRAMS

How do you become an expert in your product or service? Start with your own company's literature or training course. If your company is spending thousands, even millions, of dollars to increase your knowledge, you might as well take advantage of it. Look at your product the way a soldier looks upon his rifle: You need to know it backward and forward, eyes open or blindfolded, because your life (your livelihood) depends on it.

But knowing everything about your product doesn't mean that you have to tell everything to every client on every sales call. Too many technical details will confuse your prospects. Customers don't want to know how an air conditioner works; they just want to know it will keep them cool on hot summer days.

Instead, make recommendations and wait for customer questions. Just be sure that you know the answers. If you need some help beyond the standard sales literature, go to experts in your own company. If you sell computer systems, for example, ask your technical people any questions you're likely to hear from your customers.

You need to know your product backward and forward, eyes open or blindfolded, because your life (your livelihood) depends on it.

EVERY MINUTE COUNTS

But you need to go beyond your own company's resources when you seek product knowledge. Read everything that pertains to your business. I read all the important books relating to life insurance, estate planning and taxation in addition to every journal in my field. When I put on a seminar, I can answer every question I get with no hesitation because I know my business.

Look for articles about your competitors as well as about your own company. Make time—when you're not on calls—to do your reading. When you're on a call, take a book or journal with you. If you're stuck in a waiting room, you can turn lost time into productive time.

Beyond reading, you should regularly attend seminars and sales meetings. Not only can you learn from the presentations; you can meet other attendees and successful people in your field, and you can pick their brains. You'll hear the "inside baseball" stories not found in textbooks. Industry meetings are neutral ground, so you can even ask competitors for selling tips. Everybody—competitor or not—likes to be asked the question "How have you become so successful?"

In some cases, it's appropriate to shop for a competitor's product. If you sell Cadillacs, go to a Lincoln showroom. Take a test drive, read the literature and ask how Lincolns are better than Cadillacs. Once you know what points your competition stresses, you'll be able to tailor your own sales presentation.

If a customer says "I want to shop around," you can answer, "Why bother?" You can welcome questions about your competition and conclusively show why your product is best, as long as you've done your homework.

WINE CONNOISSEURS

How can industry knowledge work to your advantage? Take the case of Fetzer Vineyards, founded back in 1958 by Barney Fetzer, a lumber industry worker who was so strong-willed that he once threw a chair through his family television set because he thought his kids were watching too much. Barney started his enterprise on 750 acres of land with more poison oak than water.

He and his wife had 11 children, each of whom had to devote time to the family business. For example, John, the oldest son, got up at 5:00 A.M. to do chores before high school and then drove a delivery truck to the San Francisco airport after school.

By the time Barney died, in 1981, Fetzer Vineyards was a going business, producing about 200,000 cases of wine a year. But the industry was crowded with high-quality, mid-sized vineyards. How could Fetzer Vineyards distinguish itself from its competitors?

Everybody—competitor or not—likes to be asked the question "How have you become so successful?"

That's where product knowledge came in. The next generation of Fetzers spotted two trends. First, they noticed that many restaurants do a poor job of matching food with wine. As restaurants increase their sales by the glass, they need to be able to recommend specific wines with certain foods, to go beyond the traditional red-with-meat, white-with-fish advice.

The second trend concerned organic gardening. With consumers growing wary about pesticides, it has become a marketing advantage to say your product is pesticide-free. Instead of chemicals, you might rely on wasps to control pests. Therefore, the Fetzers bought a huge ranch with a garden that grows about 1,000 types of fruits, vegetables, herbs and flowers, including 85 different apples and 35 figs. This produce is now grown without pesticides, herbicides or other chemicals.

Then, Fetzer worked with restaurant owners to create menu combinations of food and wines. Marriott chefs and owners from around the world toured Fetzer Vineyards, resulting in major Fetzer promotions by the hotel chain.

The payoff: Production has increased to more than 2 million cases a year. In 1992, Brown-Forman, the company that makes Jack Daniel's whiskey, purchased Fetzer's winery and some vineyards for $110 million.

So it pays to keep up with trends in your industry. Knowing what's going on helps to spark ideas. And ideas, in the end, are every salesperson's stock in trade.

SUMMING UP

- Although an understanding of human nature is vital, a truly expert salesperson has product knowledge as well.
- Sources of product knowledge include your own company's literature, books, magazines, industry seminars and information from competitors.
- When you know your product so thoroughly that you can answer all customer questions, you can close sales by recommending the product that best suits each customer's needs.
- A knowledge of industry trends can lead to big sales as surely as will a knowledge of your own product's features.

8

▼

Prospectors Go for the Gold

"Diligence is the mother of good fortune."

MIGUEL DE CERVANTES

"One should labor so hard in youth that everything one does subsequently is easy by comparison."

ASHLEY MANTAGU

Some sales managers and "experts" talk about the need to qualify prospects—that is, check a potential buyer's financial strength before trying to sell him or her anything. To me, that's nonsense. Every prospect is a potential customer. People grow, and the customer who can afford only a small house in a marginal neighborhood today may be buying a mansion tomorrow. Chevy buyers become Cadillac buyers. You never know who's going to make it.

Therefore, you should prospect as widely as possible. The more calls you make, the more appointments you'll get and the more sales you'll close. *Selling is a numbers game.*

WORK THE CROWDS

When do you prospect? That's a simple question to answer. You prospect all the time. No matter who you meet, that person is a prospect. Or he or she has a friend or a relative who's a prospect.

Do you sell life insurance? Most people need insurance, especially if they have dependents. Surprisingly, many people who genuinely need insurance don't have any or don't have enough. They think the $50,000 group term policy from their company will protect their family, even though they're sadly mistaken.

Or suppose you're a stockbroker. Not everyone needs stocks, but everyone needs some financial advice. Even the most cautious individual might want to buy a mutual fund for income, appreciation or both. A $2,000 IRA investment might be the start of a long, mutually beneficial relationship.

Or suppose you're in real estate. Everybody has to live somewhere, and many people are attracted to the idea of a bigger, newer or more conveniently located home.

The list can go on and on. No matter what you sell, you're probably running into prospects every day. The trick is to recognize them and try to open the door for a sales presentation.

You never know who's going to make it.

If you sell primarily to businesses, call on company presidents first. They aren't constrained by a budget because they answer to no one. Therefore, if you show them an idea that will make money for them, they'll buy. Or they'll pass you down to a subordinate with a strong suggestion that your product is worth buying.

DOOR OPENERS

You probably won't have much success prospecting if you tell people you want to sell them something. Instead, tell them of your expertise: "I'm in real estate. Lately I've been doing a lot of work involving income-ᵣroducing property, bought at distress prices." If they show any interest, you might ask if you can come by and share an idea with them. Most people like to share ideas, if they're coming from you.

Strike up a conversation. Exchange business cards. Then, a few days later, you can give the prospect a call and suggest an appointment.

That doesn't mean your prospecting is limited to people you run into on an airplane or in the supermarket. Sometimes you'll get leads from your company—people who answered a newspaper ad, for example, or who responded to a direct-mail campaign. There are plenty of lists for sale, too.

An effective prospecting technique is to look for names of people mentioned in your local newspaper or trade magazines. Give them a call and congratulate them; then try for an appointment. "I saw where you were just named chief financial officer. That's great news. Have you thought yet how that will affect your family's financial situation? I have a few ideas I'd like to share with you. Maybe next Thursday at 7:00 or 8:00 A.M.?"

As you can imagine, such prospecting is best done by phone. Once you're finished with one call, you can go right on to the next. Your object generally will be to get an appointment or perhaps to get the prospect's permission to send out some product information. The more calls you make, the more appointments you'll get, even if your success ratio is only 1:10 or 1:20.

Selling is a numbers game.

OPEN FOR INSPECTION

If you know where to look, there are many prospect lists available, either for free or for a nominal cost. Sources for prospect lists include the following:

- *Political contributors.* State governments will provide you with lists of all contributors to political campaigns, including home addresses, professions and amounts contributed. If you're selling big-ticket items, for example, contributors of over $500 or $1,000 may be good prospects.

- *Registered voters.* You can get this data, by precinct, from the registrar of voters.
- *Parents of schoolchildren.* Public school directories provide leads for products such as life insurance, encyclopedias, mutual funds to save for college, etc.
- *Proxies from publicly traded companies.* These documents list top executives, along with the towns where they live.
- *Chamber of commerce member booklets.* These are great sources if you're trying to reach business owners. Some chambers of commerce sponsor mixers where you can meet members face-to-face.
- *Obituaries.* I certainly don't recommend preying on widows and widowers, but some of them desperately need assistance dealing with housing, insurance, investments, etc.
- *Alumni publications.* These publications often tell what's happening with graduates by year, so you can tell who's likely to be starting a career, who's ready to retire and so on.

NIP AND TUX

Prospecting was one of the lessons Judy Sims learned while she was attending Texas Tech University. One summer she worked in a tuxedo rental shop in Fort Worth. Rather than just waiting for customers to come in, Sims read the social pages of the local newspapers. She saw which couples had announced engagements and then cold-called them to suggest they rent formal wear for their weddings.

Ten years later Sims and her husband started a computer software store in a strip mall. Six weeks into their new business, they were going nowhere fast and were about to lose their $40,000 investment. At this point, Judy Sims remembered her college experience with cold calls. She started phoning local businesses to offer her business-oriented software. One of those calls was to Ross Perot's Electronic Data Systems, which became a major account.

People like to share ideas.

Another ten years later, the Sims' company, Software Spectrum, Inc., uses telemarketing to sell business software nationwide. Sales are over $160 million a year, profits are over $4 million and Sims is a multimillionaire. "You've got to set clear goals and stay focused," she says.

PLAYING THE PERCENTAGES

One prospecting technique that works is to set a certain amount of prospecting that you do every day, every week, every month and every year. It takes discipline, but it will pay off if you stay with it.

Let's say that you decide to make 10 cold calls every day. If you run into a busy day and make only 7 cold calls, you make 13 cold calls the next day, and so on. The trick is to make sure that you make 50 cold calls a week. Typically, your cold calls will be by phone, although you might send letters instead and then follow up on the letters. If you make 50 cold calls a week, you might wind up with five appointments a week and one sale. After a year you'll have 50 customers.

A successful salesperson will keep 90 percent of his or her customers through good service, so you'll probably keep 45 of those customers in the second year plus another 50 new ones. That's 95 customers. After three years, you'll have 140 customers, and so on. It won't be long before you have hundreds of satisfied customers, and you'll be reaping renewal business each year. What's more, *satisfied customers are great sources for referrals*. If you ask them if they can help you, they'll probably give you the names of friends or relatives you can call.

When you're calling referred leads, your batting average should be much higher than one in ten. If you raise that to only two out of ten, that's 100 new customers a year, and your referrals will increase geometrically. The more referred leads you get, the better your batting average on cold calls and the faster your customer list will grow.

Satisfied customers are great sources for referrals.

SUMMING UP

- Selling is a numbers game. The more cold calls you make, the more appointments you'll get, and the more sales you'll close.
- Don't try to qualify prospects. Sell to anyone who will buy, even if you make small sales. You never know which customers will grow to become major accounts.
- Set a certain number of cold calls to make each week.
- Ask your customers for referrals, which will increase your success ratio on cold calls.

9

▼

An Ounce of Preparation

"A man's accomplishments in life are the cumulative effect of his attention to detail."

JOHN FOSTER DULLES

"The battle of Waterloo was won on the playing fields of Eton."

ARTHUR WELLESLEY, DUKE OF WELLINGTON

It's not just in diplomacy and war that preparation is vital. Any football coach will tell you that games are won during the week, not on Saturday or Sunday. Before you win, you need good practices.

The same is true in selling. Even after you have lined up an appointment and have all the necessary product knowledge at your fingertips, you can't just saunter into a prospect's office and expect to close sales. First, you need a plan. *When you fail to prepare, you prepare to fail.*

ON YOUR OWN

Before you develop a plan, you need to face the fact that you'll be on your own when you make a sales call. You, by yourself, have to get yourself ready for each call. That's not easy for a lot of young salespeople. All their lives, they've had parents, teachers and coaches telling them what they should do. Then they go out and join a company and expect the sales manager to tell them what to do.

When you fail to prepare, you prepare to fail.

By all means, listen to your sales manager. But you'll never sell and grow rich if you expect your manager to spell it all out for you. You've got to work on your own, developing the particular talents the Lord gave you to the maximum.

I learned to rely on myself after my parents died, when I was young. When I began selling, I knew I had to push myself to the limit and work as hard as I could in order to succeed. I had to prepare myself for each sales call.

To see how important self-reliance can be, look at the career of football coach John Gagliardi. He's been a head coach for 44 seasons—40 of them at St. John's University, Collegeville, Minnesota. He's had only two losing seasons, and he's won nearly 300 games, which is the fifth highest career total among all U.S. college coaches. Playing in NCAA Division III (no athletic scholarships), his teams have gone to the national play-offs ten times and have won three national championships.

What makes Gagliardi unique? His teams have no tackle scrimmaging ("they serve mainly to keep players banged up and sore") and no wind sprints, laps, outdoor practices in bad weather, compulsory weight lifting or practices longer than 90 minutes. When the players watch game films, it's only of successful plays. (Gagliardi says; "Positive examples are the best teaching aids.")

How does St. John's win without the running and long practices? Coach Gagliardi expects his players to get themselves in shape and keep themselves there. "You're supposed to learn self-sufficiency in college," he says. "Mama's not here to tell you to study, and a coach shouldn't be there telling you to keep in shape."

The same advice applies to salespeople, young and old. It's up to you, not your manager, to do the precall preparation it takes to get to the top and stay there.

I'd imagine my presentation, his or her questions or objections, my answers and, at the end, a successful closing of the sale.

IMAGE OF A SALE

One technique I've always used extensively is "imaging." I close my eyes, clear out all the unnecessary thoughts and form a mental image of myself succeeding at a given task. Before a tennis match, for example, I imagine my serve, my opponent's return, my own ground strokes, my rush to the net and so on. I think of everything my opponent is apt to do, picturing it in my mind. Then I see myself countering my opponent's efforts, winning points and winning the match. When it comes time to play, I seem to automatically do what I've imagined myself doing. When my opponent hits a certain stroke, I immediately move to the ball and hit an effective return. My game improves by 100 percent.

My sales game improves by 100 percent when I practice imaging, too. That's something I have done right from the beginning of my career. If I were selling by phone, I'd close my eyes and imagine myself dialing the call. I'd "hear" the receptionist answer, tell her who I was and get through to the boss. Then I'd imagine my presentation, his or her questions or objections, my answers and, at the end, a successful closing of the sale.

The same was true when I'd have a personal call lined up. On my way to the prospect's office, I'd pull my car to the side of the road and sit there, visualizing the call. I'd see myself in my good suit, looking my best, smiling at the receptionist and entering the prospect's office, radiating self-confidence. I'd give the prospect a firm handshake, find a seat in his or her office and take out the yellow legal pad I always use. Then I'd go through my entire presentation in my mind, with the prospect telling me what was on his or her mind and my suggesting the product to meet the prospect's need.

Naturally, when I visualized these sales, they were always successful. More often than not, the subsequent real sales call would be a success, too.

ACTION, REACTION

There's no great mystery as to why imaging is so successful, on a sales call as well as on the playing field. For one reason, imaging is a way of planning your strategy. You can think of what your opponent, or your prospect, is likely to do and how you'll react. Then, when you're on a real call or in a real game, you're prepared for what takes place.

This is similar to the war-gaming strategy military experts have used for years. They prepare "scenarios" the enemy might come up with and how to counter them. Similarly, football coaches tirelessly review opponents' game films to try to see what plays the other team is most apt to run in certain situations. Then they devise the appropriate defensive strategies.

The more you think you can do something, the more it's likely to actually come to pass.

Planning works in sales calls, too. By imaging, you can anticipate the prospect's most likely objections—for example, "I already have enough life insurance" or "I can't afford it." By planning, you know how you'll react. You won't be caught by surprise, stumbling around for an answer that will, when it finally comes out, convince no one.

But there's more to imaging than just planning. There's also the concept of positive reinforcement. The more you think you can do something, the more it's apt to come to pass. Your mind is an incredibly powerful tool, once you really learn how to use it.

In one experiment, for example, schoolchildren were split into three groups and tested on their ability to shoot basketball foul shots. After the test, one group did nothing while another group practiced foul shots for 30 days. The third group didn't shoot any foul shots in the 30-day period. However, these children sat at their desks for 30 minutes each day, with their eyes closed, and imagined themselves shooting foul shots.

After the 30 days were up, the children were retested. As you'd expect, the group who practiced did much better, while the nonshooters had made no significant improvement. What was startling, though, was that the group who been imaging successful foul shots improved greatly, too. These children saw themselves succeeding; then they went out and did it.

That's how imaging can work for you. When you mentally see yourself making sales over and over, your mind gets the idea that you will make sales. And you will.

SUMMING UP

- You need to prepare for successful sales calls.
- Once you're in a prospect's office, you're on your own, so it's up to you to be certain you're adequately prepared.
- By imaging—going through a sale in your mind—you can anticipate any objections a prospect might raise.
- Imaging a sale in advance gets your mind thinking positively, a key ingredient for success in selling.

Your mind is an incredibly powerful tool, once you really learn how to use it.

10

▼

Face-to-Face

"You may buy land now as cheap as stinking mackerel."

WILLIAM SHAKESPEARE, *Henry IV*

Price isn't everything. It's nice to have a product that's less expensive than competitors' or one that's competitive. But people won't buy what you're selling just because it has a low price. To be an effective salesperson, you need to learn what the prospect truly wants and then offer a product to satisfy that desire. In short, you need to make an effective sales presentation.

Some salespeople think the purpose of a presentation is to bombard the prospect with information about their product or service. Or maybe they think a presentation is to announce something new—a new product, new application, new discount, etc. If the presentation interests the buyer, the seller can negotiate price and make the sale.

That may work for beginning salespeople who need a rehearsed presentation that is provided by their company or manager. Once you have a little experience, though, you'll learn how to use a "discovery" process before launching into your presentation.

I begin each sales call with my warm-up, in which I describe myself and my accomplishments so the customer will know he or she can trust me. Then I compare myself to a physician, saying, "I need to diagnose your present condition. Then I'll prescribe something for you. If it fits your philosophy and your pocketbook, fine. If not, I'll be on my way."

Most prospects agree—after all, they've agreed to the appointment. My "diagnosis" consists of asking a series of questions about the client's attitude toward life insurance:

"Do you have strong feelings about life insurance?"
"How do you feel about life insurance as an investment?"
"How do you feel about life insurance as a means of providing money for your children's education or your own retirement?"

We've become a nation of speakers who don't listen.

As you can see, I don't ask questions that can be answered with a simple yes or no. I ask prospects how they feel about things, looking for lengthy answers. I want to get my clients talking because *that's how I'll pick up clues as to what they want to buy.*

Often I start the question-and-answer session with a fairly difficult question. That requires the prospect to think a bit, setting the tone and seriousness of the interview. After I've loosened him or her up with some financial questions, I ask some that are more personal:

"Do you have a good marriage?"
"Have you had any problems with the IRS?"
"Are your kids doing all right in school?"

After I ask these questions, I don't press the prospect. I give him or her lots of time to talk, I sit back and I listen. One question I always ask is, "How did you get into your field?" Most people enjoy talking about their careers, and their responses give me many clues about their personalities.

If a prospect doesn't answer a question right away, *don't jump in to fill the silence.* In most cases, the client is simply taking his or her time to consider the answer. If you're patient, you'll get to hear from the prospect.

GO WITH THE FLOW

When you go to a doctor, you expect him or her to ask you what's wrong. You might, for example, say that you have an earache. If so, you don't want the doctor to say, "No, you have a stomachache."

The same is true for salespeople. Ask the prospect what he or she wants and then listen. If the client says she wants one thing, don't interrupt and tell her she really wants another.

LISTEN UP

When you were in school, you probably took a speech or public-speaking course. But I'll bet you never took a course in listening. As a result, *we've become a nation of speakers who don't listen.* That's why there are so many divorces, lawsuits and general misunderstandings.

Salespeople are not exceptions to this rule. Most salespeople stick to their canned presentation; they try to dominate the consumer. In short, they're determined to *sell.* Most often this type of salesperson doesn't sell much of anything.

The great salespeople I know are all listeners. They not only listen; they pay attention to what the customer is saying. They're trying to discover what the customer's problems are and pick up clues about what they can sell. As co-founder Herbert Marcus said, "There is never a good sale for Neiman-Marcus unless it's a good buy for the customer."

When you start out, a prepared presentation is a good track to run on.

Suppose, for example, a client's answers frequently refer to money problems—for example, his auto insurance just went up or his public schools aren't good so he's had to pay thousands of dollars a year for private school. This client probably doesn't have a lot of extra money to spend, so he's apt to be a prospect for term insurance, economy models, etc.

On the other hand, suppose the client mentions the expensive vacations he takes every year and his worries about his inability to build up a retirement fund. This client may have ample income but lack the discipline for saving, so he's a prospect for cash-value insurance, a mutual fund with an automatic deposit program.

Or suppose a prospect keeps talking about her children and their schooling. "My daughter goes to a fine private school," "Our local school district is considered the best in the state," "My son wants to go to an Ivy League school, but I don't know whether his SATs will be high enough," etc. This lets you know that education is extremely important to that prospect. You have a great opportunity to suggest an encyclopedia, a personal computer, magazine subscriptions, investment vehicles that can help pay for college and other items.

Sometimes a client will say, "Your product sounds great, but that's not my big headache now." To a salesperson, that's an invitation to ask what the real problem is. You may get an opening to suggest a product or service that can address the real problem.

BUY-IT-YOURSELF

Once you've discovered what a prospect really wants, you can make a recommendation. Often the prospect will want to be reassured. "Do you think that's a good mutual fund?" or "Do you really think that's a safe place to put money now?" If you merely answer "yes," that doesn't help much. You're just a salesperson trying to get a commission. But if you respond with a solid fact—"This fund has been up eight years in a row, even in 1987, when the market crashed"—that's a valid way to answer the question and reassure the prospect. Best of all, you can say, "I've got my own money in it" or "I've put my mother in it." Then the client knows that you *really* believe in your product.

If you don't believe in your products enough to buy them, you're lying to your clients on every sales call.

Don't lie to your clients; don't say you own your product if you don't. The truth always catches up to liars. Instead, put your own money into your products, unless it's inappropriate. *If you don't believe in your products enough to buy them, you're lying to your clients on every sales call.* You're better off finding something else to sell.

STICK TO BUSINESS

In an ideal sales call, you discover what the client wants and recommend a product that meets his desire. After you answer a few questions, you close the sale.

Unfortunately, sales calls are seldom ideal. If you're in the prospect's office, for example, the phone might ring with a critical call from his production manager, or his secretary will interrupt your sales call with a matter that "can't wait."

Unless you're a true pro, you've lost the sale. Your prospect's concentration will go elsewhere, and your presentation becomes unimportant. Therefore, you must reestablish the importance of the call as soon as possible. Reiterate, "So you're concerned that you won't be able to save enough money to provide you and your wife with a comfortable retirement income." Such an approach will remind the client that you're there to meet one of his vital needs.

It's even better to try to head off such problems before they occur. When I begin a sales call, I say to the prospect, "Please ask your secretary to hold all calls, but have her available in case we need any specific information."

Sometimes it's the prospect himself who tries to throw you off the track, perhaps because he's subconsciously reluctant to make a decision. He'll ask you if you want something to eat or drink; he'll show you his tropical fish tank or pictures of his daughter's wedding.

Your natural inclination is to be polite and to go along with his suggestions. That's a mistake—you want to keep control of the sales call. I never accept any kind of food or drink, even a drink of water. If a prospect wants to show me something not related to my call, I'll say something like this: "Let's focus on your family's financial security now, while we're thinking about it. Afterwards, I'll look at your pictures."

People won't buy what you're selling just because it has a low price.

PARTICIPATION, NOT DEMONSTRATION

The problem of keeping the client focused isn't as serious if you're selling a tangible piece of equipment, such as a laptop computer or a camcorder. In this case, you can have the prospect operate the equipment, focusing attention on your product. Once your prospect gets the idea that she's working it, she'll be reluctant to let go, and you can proceed to the close. This technique certainly is much more effective than doing the demonstration yourself while the prospect watches.

On the other hand, don't haul around a lot of unnecessary equipment to your sales calls. Audiovisual presentations can be complicated and dull. I seldom take anything with me but a pencil and a legal pad. I've learned how to write upside down, so I can explain things to my prospects while we're face-to-face. (If I'm calling on a prospect at home, I ask husband and wife to sit side by side, so I can cover both with one presentation.)

MARCHING ORDERS

One presentation technique I often use is to give minor "orders" to my prospects throughout the sales call. "Let me see a copy of your will," I might say, or "Take a look at these projected cash values." The idea is to get the prospect used to the idea of doing what I say. Then he or she will be more likely to go along when I say "Just sign right here" or "Make the check out to ABC Life Insurance Company."

SUMMING UP

- A good presentation begins with a series of open-ended questions, so you can get clues about the client's needs.
- If you really believe in what you sell, you should buy it. That will reassure your clients that your product really is worthwhile.
- Try to keep your client from being interrupted during a call. If an interruption does occur, get the call back on track as soon as possible.
- If you're selling equipment, have your client operate it during the sales call. Don't demonstrate it yourself while the prospect watches.
- By giving your prospect modest orders during a presentation, you'll condition the prospect to go along with your suggestion that he or she sign the sales documents.

▼▼▼

I want to get my clients talking because that's how I'll pick up clues as to what they want to buy.

11

▼

Clearing the Hurdles

"I have yet to encounter that common myth of weak men, an insurmountable barrier."

JAMES LANE ALLEN

"No task's too steep for human wit."

HORACE

"A great pilot can sail even when his canvas is rent."

SENECA

"When prospects find something wrong with what you're selling, they're finding something wrong with you." This last quote doesn't come from an ancient Roman; it comes from a modern Sicilian-American: Joe Gandolfo. When you do all the things I've advised—that is, learned your product, prospected and listened to the client and recommended a product that meets the prospect's expressed needs—and the client raises an objection, that generally means one thing. The client is saying "I don't trust you."

That's not an easy hurdle to overcome. Nevertheless, you can do it. Handle the objections calmly and pleasantly as you look the client straight in the eye. Express conviction without being too aggressive. Convey that you really care about the prospect. If you do all of these

things, you can regain the lost trust and convince the client to buy from
you.

TECHNIQUES FOR HANDLING
COMMON OBJECTIONS

"I Want To Think It Over"

Don't take tomorrow for an answer. A lot of prospects will say "I
want to think it over. Can you call me in a couple of days?" You'll
naturally want to go along with their wishes, but don't. Callbacks
generally don't pay off.

If you know your business, you're doing everything you can to make
a sale on the first call. You're finding out what the prospect wants and
recommending something to satisfy those wants. You're giving him the
reasons to buy right away. What could possibly happen in a few days
to make him want to buy then, if he doesn't want to buy now?

---

*If a prospect doesn't answer a question right away, don't jump
in to fill the silence.*

When you get this objection, ask the question "What additional
information do you hope to learn to help you make a decision?" In other
words, you tell the client that he knows as much about your product
now as he ever will. Waiting won't help him make a more informed
decision.

You also can point out that successful people make decisions when
the relevant information is fresh in their minds. Very few people can
retain information for more than a few hours. After a day, most people
retain only 75 percent of what they learned and only 50 percent after
two days. You can tell the prospect that you'll be glad to supply any
further details he needs to make a decision.

Some people are natural procrastinators. An individual who makes
hundreds of decisions every day on the trading floor of the commodities
exchange may not be able to decide which necktie to wear to work.
Such people need a push from a confident, decisive salesperson.

You might say, "Whatever you do, buy or not buy, you're making a decision today. Does it make sense to expose your family to your death or illness when you could protect them for a few thousand dollars that you really won't miss?"

"I Want To Shop Around"

This is a sure sign that the client has lost trust in you. The best counter-response you can make is to come out and ask, "Don't you trust me? Don't you think I'm being honest with you? If you trust me, we can do business now." After saying this, wait for the prospect to respond, no matter how long it takes.

"I Want To See My Friend (Or Relative) Who's in the Business"

In this case, you can point out that it's awkward to do business with a friend or relative. If you have a problem, you may be reluctant to bring it up with someone you know well. Also, you can make the point that most people don't like to have friends or relatives know their confidential financial or personal matters, which often have to be revealed when a major purchase is made.

"I Can't Afford It"

You can ask if spending the money in question really would make a difference in the client's life-style. If so, trade down to a lower-priced alternative. Over the years you may be able to trade the client up.

When prospects find something wrong with what you're selling, they're finding something wrong with you.

"Your Price Is Too High"

You can respond by saying, "Would you take my product if it were free? I'll show you how my product will pay for itself when you buy from me. Thus, you'll get it for free." Then you can show how your product will save the customer time, labor, other costs, etc.

"I Want To Talk It Over with My Spouse"

When you hear this at the end of the sales call, it's too late to do anything, unless the spouse is nearby. You're better off asking if the spouse's input is necessary when you first make the appointment. If so, ask to meet with both at the same time.

"I Never Do Business with a Stranger on the First Call"

I always answer this by saying "We stopped being strangers as soon as I walked through the door." Then I go on with the sale.

READING BETWEEN THE LINES

Sometimes you answer one objection, and the prospect poses another objection and then another. Often this is a sign that you haven't discovered the real objection. It may be that money is tight, yet the prospect doesn't want to admit it. Or the prospect may not be authorized to make a purchasing decision without approval from someone else.

You'll never close the sale until you find out the true problem, so you might as well ask, "What's really the reason you're reluctant to buy?" To help me find out, I'll add, "You do trust me, don't you?"

If the objection isn't strongly voiced, you can just ignore it. Suppose the prospect says, "I ought to think this over." You might nod your head in agreement or say you understand and then go on with the sale: "When were you born? Can I have your doctor's name?"

Don't take tomorrow for an answer.

TURNING THE TABLES

Sometimes you can use a little jujitsu and go right from an objection into a close. Suppose the buyer asks what will happen if he or she becomes disabled, can't work and thus can't keep paying the premiums. You can say, "So your only objection is your fear of not being able to pay premiums in case of disability?"

As you can see, you're rephrasing the question, making it seem as if this objection were the *only* one. Then you go on to counter the objection: "We can give you a rider that will waive premiums if you're disabled." Now you've removed the buyer's only objection, so there's nothing to stop you from closing the sale.

CONVEY CONFIDENCE

The best way to handle objections is to prevent them from ever arising. As I've said, if you're at peace with the Man Upstairs and you concentrate on the prospect's problems, you'll get him or her to trust you, and objections won't arise.

At the same time, you'll forestall objections if you act self-confident and decisive. Your prospect will pick up your behavioral pattern and make a decision right away, rather than procrastinating. If you've done your homework well, that decision will be to buy from you.

SUMMING UP

- If a prospect raises objections, that usually means he or she doesn't trust you.
- To rebuild that trust, answer each objection calmly and sincerely.
- There are a few common objections that you should learn how to answer.
- Repeated objections may be a clue to a hidden problem that you'll need to discover.

- You can turn an objection into a close by casting it as the only objection and then answering it.

Point out that successful people make decisions when the relevant information is fresh in their minds.

12

▼

Finishing Touches

"It is not by strength, but art, obtains the prize,
And to be swift is less than to be wise."

ALEXANDER POPE, *The Iliad of Homer*

A lot of books and articles about selling emphasize the close. Good salespeople, it is said, use sophisticated strategies for closing a sale, while novices never get around to asking for the order and thus never make any sales. When I run seminars on selling, I get more questions on closing than on anything else.

This focus on the close is misplaced. Sales are made or lost earlier, much earlier. *If you haven't succeeded in getting the prospect to trust you—if you've sent the wrong nonverbal signals— you won't close the sale, no matter what kind of closing line you use.*

If you haven't looked the prospect directly in the eye and listened carefully to what she has to say, you've lost her. She thinks you're peddling snake oil rather than a truly helpful product or service. The prospect may be tactful and say, "I want to shop around," but what she's really saying is, "I don't trust you."

It all comes back to the fundamentals. You have to be at peace with God, with your family and with yourself. You have to ask questions and then listen, so the prospect will tell you what she wants to buy from you. And you have to be genuinely interested in helping your prospects as human beings. When your fundamentals are in place, you'll close sales automatically.

HEADS YOU BUY, TAILS I SELL

That being said, there are ways to help you close. First of all, you have to know when to close. Don't procrastinate. Some salespeople are so comfortable with their sales presentations that they want them to go on forever. They fear rejection if they go for the close, and they don't want to ruin the cozy friendship that has built up between salesperson and client.

"Would you take my product if it were free?"

The object of making a sales call is to make a sale, not to make a presentation. After you have discovered the client's desires, suggested an appropriate product and handled the client's objections, it's time to close the sale.

I've found several techniques useful. One is to avoid giving the prospect a yes-no option. Don't say "Do you want to buy this policy?" If the prospect says no, you've lost the sale. Instead, give the prospect a yes-yes option. You might, for example, tell the prospect that a $100,000 policy will cost $2,000 a year while a $200,000 policy will cost $4,000 as year. Then you can say, "Which figure best fits your present financial situation?"

No matter how the prospect answers this question, you can proceed as if he has said yes to buying a policy. This technique is known as implied consent. After you have this implied consent, you can go ahead and ask the questions you'd ask after a sale is closed. What's your full name? Your spouse's full name? Date of birth? And so on. And, of course, you tell the prospect how large a check to write and to whom. Then . . . shut up. *A lot of salespeople lose sales at this stage because they talk too much.*

FROM THE MINORS TO THE MAJORS

You can look at the implied consent strategy as using a series of minor closes that lead to a major close. Suppose you don't think your client will come out and say "Yes, I'll take the car." You might lead up to the major close with one minor close after another, drawing the customer into the idea of owning the car of her choice.

> Salesperson: Do you prefer a full-sized or mid-sized car?
> Prospect: Full-sized.
> Salesperson: Which color?
> Prospect: White.
> Salesperson: Air-conditioned?
> Prospect: Yes.
> Salesperson: Power windows?
> Prospect: I prefer to roll them up or down by hand.

At some point, after the customer has visualized herself in the big, new, white car, you can hand her the form to sign "so your order can be processed." You have moved her from a minor to the major close. All she has to do is sign, and she'll get all the features she really wants.

You'll forestall objections if you act self-confident and decisive.

ASSUME THE BEST

Have you ever called an airline to ask for flight information? After you've learned what the schedule is from Atlanta to Denver, the telephone representative will say, "Do you want to put that on American Express, Visa or MasterCard?" The airline representative is using a technique called *assuming the sale*. The path of least resistance for you to take is to specify a credit card—in fact, confirming the sale.

Or when you pull into a gas station, the attendant may ask, "Fill it up with premium?" This assumes a big-ticket sale: the maximum amount of the high-priced product. It's easy for you to nod your head or grunt an affirmative. If you want to make a less expensive purchase, it's up to you to specify how many dollars' worth of regular. The ball is in your court.

For a classic example of assuming the sale, think back to the last time you went shopping for a suit. After you tried one on and were looking at yourself in the mirror, did the salesman ask, "Do you want it?" Not very likely. Instead, he probably said, "You look great in this suit." Then he made some adjustments, saying, "We'll just take it in a bit here." And, of course, he called the tailor over for an opinion; the tailor, naturally, agreed that you looked fantastic in the suit. "We'll do this and this and this," the tailor said, making chalk marks all over the suit.

> Salesman: What do you think of the way it fits in the back?
> Tailor (making some more chalk marks): Looks good. Cuff or no cuff? (He then marks the length.)
> Salesman: How soon can you have this suit ready?
> Tailor: Next Monday.

So here you are, with a suit all marked up and ready for alteration. At this point, can you really say that you don't want the suit after all the work that's already been done? Probably not. In fact, the salesman, having assumed the sale of a suit, is probably taking you over to the accessories department to pick out a matching shirt and tie.

If you haven't succeeded in getting the prospect to trust you, you won't close the sale, no matter what kind of closing line you use.

KEEP YOUR HOPES ALIVE

Assuming a sale may be more effective than asking for an outright close. When you ask a prospect to buy, you're risking a "no," which effectively ends the presentation. Assuming the sale eases into a close.

If you don't get a good response the first time around, you can try another approach. Here are some examples of how I assume the sale in life insurance:

"What's your height and weight?"
"Who would you like to name as the beneficiary?"
"Would you prefer to pay premiums monthly or quarterly?" (As you can see, I assume the sale and gradually build up to a major commitment.)

If I have a client who needs a big policy, say $1 million or $2 million, I suggest taking the $2 million. "If the premium is too much, we can cut back after a year or so," I'll say. "After you grow older, it's always easier to decrease coverage than to increase it."

When you assume the sale, you don't say "Do you want my product?" Instead, you keep asking the client how, when and where he or she wants the product.

TUNING IN

Often a prospect will tell you she's ready to buy—ready for you to close the sale—by her actions or words. If she asks "Do you have a monthly payment plan?" or "How much will this house cost to maintain?" she's sending you a buy signal. Here are some other telltale lines:

"Is there a charge for delivery?"
"How soon can it be ready?"
"How does the warranty work?"
"May I try it on?"

When you hear questions like these, answer them and go for the close.

Actions can speak just as loud as words. The customer who keeps using the computer during a sales presentation obviously can't wait to take that computer home. The same is true with the customer who sits in the driver's seat of one particular car, swings a particular golf club or strokes a leather jacket. In each case the customer really is saying "I want to buy." So sell him what he wants.

The object of making a sales call is to make a sale, not to make a presentation.

NO TIME LIKE THE PRESENT

How do you close the sale when a client procrastinates? By building a sense of urgency. If you sell life insurance, you can indicate that your client's health may change, which will make it more expensive to buy insurance in the future. In the meantime the prospect's family is unprotected in case of an untimely death. What would happen to your spouse and children if you were killed in an auto accident tomorrow?

Other types of salespeople can build urgency among prospects. A real estate salesperson, for example, can say that the house under consideration might not be available much longer. A computer salesperson can't use that approach; instead, he or she can suggest to the prospect that shipping or inventory control or whatever is bound to get worse every day the computer isn't installed. A stockbroker, of course, can say that the price may go up while the prospect waits.

No matter what you sell, there's not only a reason to buy your product; there's a reason to buy it *now*. By emphasizing that reason, you can turn reluctant prospects into buyers.

BIDDING WARS

In some sales situations, the close involves submitting a sealed bid. As long as your product is on the approved list and meets the specs, you'll close the sale by submitting the low bid. This sounds simple, but that's far from the truth in many instances. Sealed-bid deals are often prone to manipulation, so you need to know the ground rules.

Keep your bid confidential and never submit a bid too early. There's always the chance that your bid might be opened and the number relayed to a competitor, who can undercut it. In some cases involving large contracts, it pays to have two salespeople who travel different routes submit copies of the bid in case one runs into delays.

What if a bid has to be submitted to two different places? Again, use two salespeople to deliver the bids, making sure both bids are submitted a minute or two before the deadline.

Give the prospect a yes-yes option.

PRESCRIPTION FOR SELLING

How do I close these days? Actually, I don't. Now people pay me $1,000 to come and meet with them. I act as a consultant—an analyst for their financial situation. I listen to what they have to say and make recommendations.

Then I turn them over to two specialists who work for me. One covers life insurance and retirement plans; the other handles investments, such as mutual funds and annuities. If the client wants to take my advice—advice the client has already paid for—he or she can buy from my specialists.

I liken myself to a general practitioner who takes blood samples, urine samples, etc., and then tells the patient to see a urologist. If the patient wants to follow up, fine. Most of them do because they respect my judgment and know I have their best interests at heart. They've paid me for my time, so they know I'll be objective. I won't put a gun to their heads and tell them what to do or what to buy.

My recommendations aren't just in the areas of life insurance and annuities. I'll tell clients whether they need a prenuptial agreement, a living trust or whatever. If they need me to recommend a good lawyer, I'll do it. If they decide not to do anything . . . well, I tell them I'll love them anyway. Most of all, I tell my clients to do whatever makes them feel comfortable. If you have peace of mind, you'll live longer, no matter what else you do.

My staff and I do a lot of "witnessing," too. Prospects and clients tell us about their illnesses, their family problems and so on. Perhaps they're in bankruptcy or they're being sued. More often than you think, they don't have anyone else to talk to. They're lonely, especially the older people.

What do we tell them? Turn to God. Once you're at peace with the Man Upstairs, everything else will follow. With this kind of advice, we not only close sales; we hold onto our clients many years afterward.

SUMMING UP

- Closing the sale is not as important as some salespeople think it is. If you have your fundamentals in place, closing will follow naturally from your sales presentation.
- When you have proposed a suitable product and answered any objections, go into your close without procrastinating.

A lot of salespeople lose sales at the close because they talk too much.

- Instead of offering the prospect a yes-no choice, suggest two choices, either of which results in a sale for you.
- With the implied consent or assumed sale techniques, you proceed as if the customer has said yes, without ever actually asking whether the prospect wants to buy.
- If you ask a series of minor, innocuous questions, you can lead the conversation with the prospect into agreement to a major commitment.
- Sometimes a prospect's words or actions can send a signal that he or she is ready to buy.
- If a client procrastinates, you can close the sale by giving an urgent reason to act right away.

13

The End Is Just
the Beginning

"In this business, you can never wash the dinner dishes and say they're done. You have to keep washing them constantly."

MARY WELLS LAWRENCE

You probably get any number of mail solicitations for magazines and newsletters. Publishers routinely send them out by the thousands. That's how they get subscribers.

There's a rule of thumb in this industry. When you solicit subscribers in the mail, you try to break even. That is, if you spend $1 million on a mailing, you try to attract $1 million in subscriptions. How can this make economic sense? Say your newsletter charges $100 a year. If you received $1 million in subscriptions, that's 10,000 subscribers.

After a year you'll send out a letter asking subscribers to renew. If your publication is any good, you'll get 50 percent, 60 percent or even 80 percent renewals. Thus, for about $3,000 worth of postage to those 10,000 subscribers, you might get $500,000 in renewals. The $1 million you invested in year 1 might earn you $500,000 in year 2, $400,000 in year 3, etc., if your renewal rate holds up.

Assuming the sale eases into a close.

DEFERRED GRATIFICATION

What's the message here? Getting a customer is only the beginning. For all types of salespeople, the big payoff may come afterward. You might get commissions on annual renewals, upgrades to higher-commission products or referrals to more prospects. No matter what you sell, every customer you add to your list is a valuable resource. Top salespeople expect 80 percent of their sales income to come from referrals and repeat business.

How can you mine your customer base most effectively? In a word, *service*. The more you service your clients, the greater the long-term payoff. That's true no matter what you sell. A lot of salespeople are out there, and they have products or services similar to yours. The only way you can keep your clients from your competitors is to provide them with better service.

As I've indicated earlier, I send a handwritten letter to every new client immediately after the sale to congratulate him or her. That helps them deal with buyer's remorse; most buyers like to get positive reinforcement that they've done the right thing.

SEASON'S GREETINGS

I also send my clients birthday cards and Christmas cards. Even my wealthiest clients—successful professionals or business owners who own luxury cars and vacation around the world—have told me how much they like getting those cards. Most people get no more than a handful of birthday cards each year. All you have to do is find out your client's date of birth when you make the sale and then send out a card at the appropriate time.

I also call each client at least once a year, on the anniversary of the first policy he or she bought from me. As an insurance salesman, there are things I need to keep up with: births or deaths of relatives, marriages or divorces, increases in the value of a business, etc. At the same time, I keep clients up to date with tax law and estate planning strategies, which change almost every year.

I even send out a monthly tax letter to my clients to update them on recent developments. In addition, I send out copies of magazine and newspaper articles that might be important to certain clients. And I send thank-you notes to anyone who gives me a referral, whether or not it results in a sale.

Often a prospect will tell you when he or she is ready to buy.

FOREVER YOURS

I tell my clients I'll be there for them when they need me, not when it's convenient for me. Therefore, I'm on call 24 hours a day, 7 days a week.

In addition, a salesperson should never sell too hard. Don't over-promise. If you don't deliver what you said you would, you won't keep your clients, no matter what you do after the sale.

TEAM BUILDING

Can you really service your clients when your customer base grows to hundreds or even thousands of people? Will you spend so much time servicing your clients that you spend less time selling—and thus less time earning money?

Not necessarily. As you add clients, you make more money. As you make more money, you can afford to hire high-quality support people. Over the years, as my client base has grown, I have gradually built up a staff to whom I delegate a lot of the customer service responsibility.

MAKE YOUR PRESENCE KNOWN

But service to the client doesn't begin then. Often, you're providing service to the client before the sale—that's why you're rewarded with a commission. It's important that you let your client know the range of service you've provided.

Suppose you're in real estate, and you're trying to sell a house for a client. Keep the client informed about all the things you're doing on his or her behalf. Call or write when you help find interested buyers, arrange to have an appraiser come over, line up a photographer, place a newspaper ad, help a buyer get a mortgage and so forth. Then, when you sell the house for $150,000, the buyer won't wonder what the real estate agent did to earn $9,000.

At the same time, you'll probably have to pass on bad news to your client, too (e.g., one buyer thought the house didn't have enough closet space, another buyer was turned down for a loan or an engineer one of the buyers hired said the house needs a new roof). No matter how bad the news, you're better off telling your client right away. When you delay, the news can only be worse. If you keep bad news from your client and a lack of follow-up action results in disaster, you'll get the blame—and rightfully so. *Bad news won't go away, but your customers might.*

There's not only a reason to buy your product; there's a reason to buy it now.

DROP THE DROP-INS

Customer service means just that: serving your clients. It doesn't mean entertaining them. (Entertaining clients can be a productive activity, but it can't replace service.) Customer service doesn't mean buying dinners and drinks for clients or telling them dirty jokes.

Your clients probably are busy people, just like you. When you drop in just to talk about inconsequential items, you're wasting your clients' time, to no one's benefit. If you do this too often, your clients will make excuses not to see you when you come around. Then, when you have something really important to say, you won't get a chance to say it.

SUMMING UP

- If you provide good service to your customers, you'll wind up with renewals and upgrades at little additional cost.
- Don't skip the basics such as post-sale thank-you letters, birthday cards and Christmas cards.
- Keep in touch with each client at least once a year.
- Give each client a number where you can be reached at any time.
- If you provide presale service, make sure your client knows what you do on his or her behalf.
- Don't put off giving bad news to your clients.
- Don't waste your clients' time by dropping in for no purpose.

▼▼▼

Every customer you add to your list is a valuable resource.

14

▼

Turn Lemons
into Lemonade

*"Mishaps are like knives, that either serve us or cut us, as
we grasp them by the blade or the handle."*

JAMES RUSSELL LOWELL

The old saying "The only things you can be sure about are death and
taxes" isn't true when it comes to salespeople. All salespeople can be
certain of something else: rejection. Nobody bats 1.000. You have to
get used to the idea that some prospects will turn you down. As long
as you have solid support from your family and a good relationship
with the Man Upstairs, you can pick yourself up and get back in the
game.

If you think there are people who always win, just look at the sports
world. Baseball's greatest hitter, Ty Cobb, got a hit less than 37 percent
of the time. Today hitters with a 30 percent success rate are paid
millions of dollars. In tennis, not even the top-ranked players win every
match. And the same is true outside of sports. Bill Cosby has had a
string of movie bombs, yet he's the world's most highly paid enter-
tainer.

Looking back through history, you'll see similar stories. Thomas
Edison recorded 25,000 failures while he was inventing the storage
battery. "Those were not failures," he said. "I just learned 25,000 ways
not to make a storage battery." Abraham Lincoln suffered one nervous
breakdown, two business failures and eight major political defeats

before going on to be a great president. And as far back as ancient Greece, Plutarch, the leading biographer of that time, noted, "Those who aim at great deeds must also suffer greatly."

THE TOUGH GET GOING

As I like to say, "Tough times never last. Tough people do." Sure, you'll have slumps—even top producers do. The key to successful selling is to cut your slumps short and let your winning streaks run. Nobody makes every sale. I learned that lesson the hard way: My first day selling, I got seven appointments and wound up with seven refusals. It happens to everyone.

I'm on call 24 hours a day, 7 days a week.

The best way to break out of a slump is to keep prospecting and making sales calls. There is no substitute for keeping busy. Sooner or later the numbers game will break in your favor, and you'll be hearing yes instead of no.

Successful salespeople don't let the disappointments get the best of them. After you lose one call, you must make another call and then another, until you keep selling. What's the alternative? Sit home and sulk? Have a few drinks? You'll just destroy yourself by thinking negative thoughts, and you'll have nothing positive to show for it.

Of course, you should work smarter as well as harder when you're in a slump. Successful salespeople not only survive rejection; they learn from it. After an unsuccessful sales call, you can replay the conversation in your mind. Try to figure out where you went wrong. Was the prospect not interested right from the beginning? Maybe you generated nonverbal cues that caused the prospect to mistrust you. Did you probe enough and try to find out what the customer wanted to buy? Is that what you offered him or her? If not, that's probably what you need to work on. Did you talk too much instead of allowing the prospect to tell you what he or she wanted to buy?

One good technique is to go over your latest *successful* call in your head to see what you did that led to a sale. There also are a few other tricks I've learned to help get over a slump. One is to give yourself a daily goal. For example, make a given number of phone calls and appointments per day. Don't go home until you've reached those goals, even if you have to work a little longer. When I started selling, I never quit work until I sold at least one policy in a day, no matter how small. Then I'd always have at least one success to look back on.

I use self-rewards and punishments, too. If I make my daily goals, I treat myself in some manner. When I started out, these rewards were simple—perhaps an extra hour of sleep or a special dessert. As I grew more successful, the rewards grew, too. For example, I'd reward myself with a pair of tennis shorts or a racquet, and I gradually built up to a new Mercedes!

On the other hand, I punish myself in some way for not meeting goals. That first day, when I was 0 for 7, I went to bed without dinner.

Bad news won't go away, but your customers might.

POSITIVE FEEDBACK

To break out of a slump, you need to bolster your mental attitude. Great basketball players are confident they'll make every shot, even though the best ones succeed only half the time. When you exude confidence, you'll make sales. If you go into a presentation with a negative attitude, the prospect will pick it up, and he or she won't buy from you. As Mary Kay Ash, chairperson of Mary Kay Cosmetics, said, "If you think you can, you can. And if you think you can't, you're right."

How can you keep that positive attitude while you're in a slump? One technique is to call on satisfied customers, to see how they're doing with the product or service they bought from you. You don't have to sell them anything; you just have to find out if they're still pleased and remind them that you're interested. Their enthusiasm will perk you up and will reassure you that you can sell successfully. Besides, you might be able to sell a new product or an upgrade while you're there, or you might get some first-rate referrals.

Talk to positive thinkers while you're in a slump. Such people might include your manager, top producers in your company or even a neighbor who has a successful career. More likely than not, they'll tell you about their own rough spots, which they've managed to overcome. You'll be inspired to go out and sell that much harder.

Another good idea is to read some books (or listen to tapes in your car) with an inspirational message. I like to read biographies of great achievers such as John Templeton, George Patton, Harry Truman, Douglas MacArthur, Bear Bryant, Vince Lombardi and John Wooden. I also read books by Billy Graham, Pat Robertson, Norman Vincent Peale, Dr. Robert Schuller and Dr. Charles Stanley. Of course, I find inspiration in the Bible as well as in *Lives of the Saints*.

There are a few movies that can inspire you, such as *Brian's Song* and *Chariots of Fire*. In my opinion, though, most of today's movies are not very good. You'll do better thinking about how you can help others—either your clients or those less fortunate than you.

Think about helping other people, not about helping yourself. When you're thinking along those lines, the Man Upstairs is on your side. You can find no greater help when you're trying to break out of a slump.

Abraham Lincoln suffered one nervous breakdown, two business failures and eight major political defeats before going on to be a great president.

SUMMING UP

- Even the best salespeople experience slumps. The most effective remedy is to keep prospecting, banking on the law of averages to bring in new business.
- When you're rejected, try to replay the sales call to see where you went off the track.
- Similarly, replay your last truly successful sales call to see what you were doing right before you went into the slump.

- Other slumpbreakers include calling on a satisfied customer, talking to top salespeople and reading inspirational books.
- Keep your focus on your customer, not yourself. When you offer customer satisfaction, you'll close sales.

▾▼▾

Tough times never last.
Tough people do.

PART THREE

Selling in the Nineties

The best way to break out of a slump is to
keep prospecting and making sales calls.
There is no substitute for keeping busy.

15

▼

Multiply and Conquer

"The moe the merrier."

JOHN HEYWOOD, *Proverbes*

If you're handy with numbers, you may be wondering how I sell over $1 billion of life insurance a year. Working 6 days a week, 52 weeks a year, that would be more than $3 million of life insurance every day. Can anyone really be that successful, that consistently?

Not if you do it the hard way. One-on-one selling was fine back in the days of silent movies and hand-cranked autos, but we've all come a long way since then. To make the most of my time, now I sell to large groups. I use a technique called *seminar selling*. I've been doing it since the mid-1970s, when I got sick and tired of knocking on doors and making phone calls. It's worked out so well that I do most of my selling this way these days.

In essence, here's how seminar selling works. I send out invitations to a conference, at which I speak. At the end of the conference, I collect cards from people who want a personal follow-up from me. When I call them later, I go over their needs carefully and make recommendations. Then my specialists sell whatever insurance, annuities or investments might be needed to implement my recommendations.

People respect you if you charge for your time.

SKIMMING THE CREAM

To make this strategy work, you have to carefully select your target audience. Otherwise, you'll waste your time speaking to people who have no need for your product or service.

I deal in sophisticated financial and estate planning strategies. Therefore, the people I want to reach are those with extensive assets and high incomes. I have nothing against blue-collar workers, but there aren't very many of them who will buy a $1 million policy from me.

You might think, Joe, you should call on doctors. They have income and assets. Actually, not only do many doctors spend almost all of what they make; they're prime targets. Everybody with something to sell—from luxury cars to condos—is out there chasing after doctors. Instead, I prefer to prospect business owners and entrepreneurs. According to *The Wall Street Journal*, 80 percent of all U.S. millionaires are business owners. While doctors are pursuing showy life-styles, business owners are building equity and thus increasing their wealth.

In recent years, I've concentrated on auto-related business owners—car dealers and people who own body shops or muffler shops. Not many salespeople focus on muffler shop owners, yet they may have net worths several times that of the average doctor.

How do you find prospects in such specialized areas? That's not too difficult. Developing mailing lists has become a huge industry in the United States. You probably realized that from all the solicitations you get in the mail every day. Well, if you call a mailing list broker, you'll probably find a list of the kinds of people you want to reach. In any sizable metropolitan area, these brokers will be listed under "mailing lists" in the local Yellow Pages.

You can use other means to attract attendees, especially if your seminar is not aimed at a specific target audience. You can appear on local radio and television call-in shows and mention your seminars. You can advertise in local newspapers, even magazines. For some of my seminars, I've advertised in *USA Today* and *The Wall Street*

FIGURE 15.1   Sample Seminar Invitation—Cover

You are cordially invited to attend a most important financial seminar

Journal. Don't be afraid of the cost; in seminar selling, you need to invest money to make money.

CATCH FLIES WITH HONEY

Once you have a list of prospects, you can invite them to hear you speak. The key is to make the seminar topic something they'll really want to find out about. A seminar entitled "Why You Need More Life Insurance" isn't likely to attract many people. But business owners probably will prize an invitation to a seminar entitled "How To Reduce Income Taxes Both Personal and Corporate while Living and How To Eliminate Estate Taxes and Probate Fees Without Buying Life Insurance or Annuities." Figures 15.1–15.4 show you some examples of my seminar invitations and ads.

Think about helping other people, not about helping yourself.

Of course, the invitation should include something about yourself and your credentials for speaking on the subject. I mention that I've

▼▼▼

Even a rose has thorns.

FIGURE 15.2   Sample Seminar Invitation—Inside Text

Joe M. Gandolfo, PhD, as seen on the CBN 700 Club for the past ten years, Christian Television Network, Eternal Word Television Network and numerous seminars across the United States and surrounding countries will talk about "How To Reduce Income Taxes Both Personal and Corporate while Living and How To Eliminate Estate Taxes and Probate Fees upon Death Without Buying Life Insurance or Annuities." He will also talk about perpetuation of your business, selling of assets without paying capital gains taxes and transferring of your assets to your loved ones tax-free. Dr. Gandolfo has been in practice for 33 years with approximately ten thousand clients in all 50 states ranging from a small net worth to a high net worth of $2 billion.

Date: Friday, December 13, 1992
Time: 9:00 A.M.–10:30 A.M.
Location: The Registry Resort, 475 Seagate Dr., Naples
Seating capacity limited to 50.
Call Kim Bauer, (800) 553-1008, for your reservation.

---

been seen on television for the past ten years, that I have presented these seminars across the United States and surrounding countries, and that I have 10,000 clients in all 50 states.

Remember, people like convenience when they shop these days. Whatever you're selling, make it easy for people to buy. When I mail out invitations to my seminar, I include a simple sign-up application (including a space for the prospect's phone number) and a postpaid return envelope. In case they don't trust the mail, I give them a toll-free phone number so that they can call to register.

I usually hold my seminars at a hotel/motel—not at a downtown luxury hotel and not in a scruffy fleabag on the wrong side of town. I like a modest, modern motel that provides easy access from major highways. Remember, your prospects want convenience.

These seminars generally take place in the morning so that business owners can attend before starting the workday. I schedule the meeting for an hour and a half; that's about as long as people will give you for this type of meeting. On the invitation, print "9:00 A.M.–10:30 A.M.," rather than just "9:00 A.M.," which leaves the time open-ended.

FIGURE 15.3   Sample Seminar Ad

FREE FINANCIAL SEMINAR

Come to the most eye opening seminar you have ever attended!

• How to Reduce Income Taxes Both Personal & Corporate While Living.

• How To Eliminate Estate Taxes And Probate Fees Upon Death Without Buying Life Insurance Or Annuities.

Joe M. Gandolfo, PhD

• Perpetuation Of Your Business, Selling Of Assets Without Paying Capital Gains Taxes And Transferring Your Assets To Your Loved Ones, <u>Tax Free</u>.

Dr. Gandolfo, has been seen on the CBN 700 Club for the past 10 years, Christian Television Network, Eternal Word Television Network and numerous seminars across the U.S.A. and surrounding countries.

FRIDAY, DECEMBER 13, 1991 9:00am - 10:30am
The Registry Resort, 475 Seagate Drive
Seating is limited - Call Kim Bauer at 1-800-553-1008

NO FOOD, MORE THOUGHT

Depending on how well you've drawn up your list and how effective the invitation is, you'll get few or many responses. In any case, you or your secretary should call to confirm the appointments. This will impress the prospect with your professionalism and increase the likelihood that your seminar is entered into the prospect's appointment book. That will make it more probable that he or she will attend the meeting.

FIGURE 15.4   Sample Seminar Flier

You are cordially invited to a special tax planning seminar for Chiropractors.

How to Reduce Income Taxes Both Personal and Corporate While Living and How to Eliminate Estate Taxes and Probate Fees Without Buying Life Insurance or Annuities

- Section 419 Benefit Plan (deduct twice your salary in one year)
- How to Make your Children's Education Tax Deductible
- Wills
- Living Trusts
- Durable Power of Attorneys
- Pre-nuptial Agreements
- Post-nuptial Agreements
- Live-in Agreements
- Asset Protection from a Divorce
- How to Protect Your Assets from Lawsuits (Malpractice)
- Deferred Compensation Plans Without Including Other Employees
- Independent Contractors
- Buy-Sell Agreements for Corporations and Partnerships
- Selling Your Practice or Real Estate with No Capital Gains Tax
- How to Perpetuate Your Estate Free of Estate Taxes Without Buying Life Insurance (Estate taxes 18-55% of your estate)
- Avoid Probate Fees (6-22% of your estate)

It's not what you make but what you keep that counts!

SPECIALIZING IN ESTATE AND FINANCIAL PLANNING FOR CHIROPRACTORS FOR THE PAST 32 YEARS

Date: Saturday, April 25, 1992
Time: 9:00 a.m. - 10:30 a.m.
Location: The Marriott Westshore,
1001 N. Westshore Blvd., Tampa, FL

Seating Capacity limited. Call Kim Bauer (800) 553-1008 for your reservation.

▼▼▼

You need to invest money to make money.

At the conference itself, be strictly businesslike. I don't serve food at my seminars; this isn't a party. As long as people in the back rows can see me, I stand on the guests' level, not on a stage, and I use a flip chart instead of a flashy slide show. I write on the flip chart as I speak, which always impresses people. Audiovisual presentations are too impersonal; I want to establish personal contact with the audience.

I don't sell life insurance at my seminars. Instead, I talk about common estate planning pitfalls and how to avoid them. Business owners may think their problems are unique in their industry, but their questions are the same. How can I cut my taxes? How can I leave my business to my kids? (They mainly have financial concerns.) I discuss sophisticated strategies such as charitable trusts and private foundations. If the audience wants to follow up, fine. If not, that's their business. I set out the whole smorgasbord of ideas and leave it up to them to decide.

I always leave lots of time for questions from the audience—say, 30 to 45 minutes. I answer all questions, and I answer them right away, without hesitation. I read three or four hours a day to keep up with my profession, and I have a photographic memory, so I remember it all. My audience likes my responses because I'm not wishy-washy. It's not easy at the beginning, but after you've been doing this for a few years, you get to hear many of the same questions, so you'll know the answers.

After the meeting, I have all the attendees fill out cards, saying whether or not they'd like a follow-up visit from me. I usually get requests from 40 to 50 percent of the audience. The issues I raise are important, and, all too often, no one else is discussing them. I charge $1,000 for these follow-up calls—just to talk with people about their financial plans. The money is nice, of course, but the impression this fee creates is just as important. People respect you if you charge for your time.

I usually follow up by phone. That's the most time-efficient way to do business, for myself and most of my clients. Maybe 40 times a year, I'll run into a situation that actually requires me to make a personal visit to a client.

Of the people who request follow-up, what percentage do I sell? Nearly 100 percent. If these people have taken a couple of hours to attend a seminar and then spent $1,000 just to talk to me, you can bet they are concerned enough about their circumstances to buy what I recommend.

Make the seminar topic appealing—something they will really want to attend.

I sell to all sorts of people this way—from owners of fairly small businesses to some very rich and famous people. I increasingly find that the very rich don't want to do business with advisers who live in their hometowns because they don't want anyone who lives locally to know their business. They like hiring out-of-town advisers, like me. Some of the richest and most famous people are so miserable that they're happy to talk with anyone who has a genuine interest in their problems, and they can tell that I'm sincere when I say I want to help.

That's how I sell now. I prospect in large numbers, qualify my prospects at seminars and sell over the phone. I sell billions of dollars of life insurance this way. Seminar selling may or may not work for your product or service, but it's probably worth a try. If you can establish yourself as an expert, buyers will come to you, instead of the other way around.

SUMMING UP

- Seminar selling can increase your reach and your earnings.
- One strategy is to invite prospects to a free seminar on a topic of interest; this should be held at a local hotel/motel.
- At the seminar, you can provide general information and answer any questions.
- Seminar attendees should be given the opportunity to request a follow-up visit from you.
- The actual sales will be made on the follow-up visits. A well-executed seminar can lead to dozens of sales.

▼▼▼

These seminars generally
take place in the morning
so business owners can
attend before starting
the workday.

16

Bridging the Gender Gap

"They talk about a woman's sphere as though it had a limit;
There's not a place in earth or heaven,
There's not a task to mankind given,
There's not a whispered 'yes' or 'no,'
There's not a life, a death, or birth,
That has a feather's weight of worth
Without a woman in it."

KATE FIELD

Today no one talks seriously about a "woman's sphere." Women are everywhere in the 1990s, especially in sales. One of my daughters, Diane, is in sales. She's a leading producer for Allstate Insurance.

A woman who truly has her fundamentals in place can be great in sales—*beauty attracts and brains sell.* From my experience, men like to do business with women. At the same time, women like to do business with women. As a general rule, people trust women more than they trust men. And if a salesperson has the buyer's trust, a signed contract won't be far behind.

In a lot of ways, selling is a great field for women. If you produce, you'll be paid accordingly. There won't be any excuses or old-boy network to contend with. In addition, in some types of selling, women have a lot of flexibility to set their own schedules. That can come in handy when you're trying to juggle work and family.

CHANGING WITH THE TIMES

For Marion McGovern, a former management consultant with Booz, Allen & Hamilton, helping women juggle work and family is a career in itself, thanks to an idea she came up with at a baby shower. The women there were educated professionals who were chiefly in their thirties. Some wanted to stay home with their babies but continue to work. Others wanted to take brief maternity leaves and then go back to their employers.

So McGovern and Paula Reynolds, an AT&T marketing manager, came up with the idea of M2—for Mother Managers. It's a temporary employment agency specializing in maternity leaves; businesswomen-mothers fill the vacancies for a few months until the maternity leave has ended. Within a few years, M2 became a million-dollar business, netting hundreds of thousands of dollars for McGovern and Reynolds, both of whom run this business while they raise their own children.

People trust women more than they trust men.

SAFETY FIRST

For a woman, there are definite advantages to being an independent rep. There's no boss to answer to and no potential conflicts with the boss's wife or girlfriend. That's often a big problem for women who are successful in business, as they may have to contend with jealousy from other women. Moreover, not having a boss cuts down your exposure to sexual harassment.

Are there risks to being in sales? Women certainly should take care not to dress flamboyantly, unless they're in a fashion or other glamour industry. They should wear conservatively cut clothes in quiet colors. You must make sure the client understands that your relationship is strictly business. You're selling a product, not yourself.

Otherwise, women in sales have many of the same concerns men have, only more so. If you spend a lot of time in your car, be sure to have a first-rate car phone that you can use in case of emergencies. The

$50 or so you pay for an AAA membership may be the best money you spend all year. And keep your car door locked at all times, with the windows up, now that carjacking is becoming a national pastime. If a car taps you lightly from behind, don't get out and check the damage until you're comfortable with the situation. That's becoming a favorite ploy for kidnappers as well as car thieves.

Be careful when you're staying in a hotel, too. Even if it's a five-star resort that's recommended in all the guidebooks, put the chain on and prop a chair under the doorknob. The hotel industry is notorious for its lack of security.

Beyond these precautions, women in sales need to have the same fundamental strengths as men do. You must be right with God, have a stable home life and maintain a positive approach to your body and your mind. Then you, too, can sell and grow rich!

If you can establish yourself as an expert, buyers will come to you, instead of the other way around.

SUMMING UP

- Sales is an excellent career for women.
- People tend to trust women, which gives them an advantage in selling situations.
- Women in sales have to be careful not to give off the wrong signals or expose themselves to dangerous situations.
- For women who are juggling both career and family, it pays to hire someone else to take care of the housekeeping.

▼▼▼

Beauty attracts and brains sell.

17

▼

Selling Goes High-Tech

"I hitched my wagon to the electron rather than to the proverbial star."

DAVID SARNOFF

In some ways, I'm very much the traditionalist in my selling. When I'm on a sales call, my main tools are a legal pad and a pencil. In my seminars, I use an old-fashioned flip chart rather than a multimedia sound-and-light show.

But that's not to say I'm wedded to the past. I use today's technology whenever it makes sense. If something makes you more productive or makes it easier for your customers to place orders, you should take advantage of it.

A car phone, for example, is a must for most salespeople. You probably spend a lot of time in your car; with a phone, you're always in reach of your office in case events break quickly and you need to be informed. You can use your phone to check in, confirm appointments or prospect while you're stuck in traffic. There's nothing that will stretch your working day more than a car phone.

Besides a phone, you should have a cassette player in your car. When you're not on the phone, you can be listening to educational cassettes, current events, etc.

Another handy device for just about everybody, but especially salespeople, is a cassette recorder. Whenever an idea strikes you—for example, a new application for your product—you can dictate into your recorder. Then have an employee transcribe your dictation so that you can see your ideas on paper and take whatever action is appropriate.

If you do a lot of business with out-of-town clients, put in a toll-free 800 line. You'd be surprised how many people, even extremely wealthy ones, don't like to pay for long-distance phone calls. If you have a toll-free phone line, they won't hesitate to call you. I get 70 to 80 calls every day on my toll-free line. Think how many sales I'd miss without it!

When you exude confidence, you'll make sales.

With a toll-free line, you'll get calls from prospects, which you can convert into sales. And you'll get calls from clients who want to upgrade the product you've already sold them. You'll also hear right away from troubled clients, so you can address their problems before they become lost causes. For any number of reasons, you're better off if your clients feel they can call you at any time, and a toll-free line will encourage that communication.

MAKE IT EASY

A toll-free line can beat the competition by offering better customer service. That's what Michael Dell was thinking back in 1984, when he was a 19-year-old college student. The IBM personal computer and its clones were then moving into virtually every home and office, but buyers had to go to a retail store. Retail stores would charge a markup for service, which often wasn't worth very much. Many customers knew more about PCs than the dealers did, and any sort of a custom order usually proved excruciating.

So Dell proceeded to take on IBM, Compaq and the rest with one arrow in its quiver—an 800 telephone line. Responding to newspaper ads, customers could call Dell, toll-free, and order directly. Buying this way was much more convenient, and the service turned out to be at least as good as retailers had to offer. Even on small custom orders, Dell could deliver service much faster than rivals could.

Dell's lean distribution structure enabled him to keep costs down, but he didn't want to sell on price alone: There's always someone out there who will cut prices below yours. Instead, he boosted customer service. He offered buyers unlimited calls to a toll-free technical support line and a 30-day, money-back guarantee. If a customer needs an on-site service call, Dell will have an independent technician there the next day—free of charge, up to one year after a purchase. If a buyer calls the Dell technical support line and doesn't speak to a rep within five minutes, the customer gets a check for $25.

Even with all this customer support, Dell Computer Company's selling and administrative expenses are only 14 cents per dollar of sales, versus 20 cents for Compaq, 24 cents for Apple and 30 cents for IBM. Dell now employs 600 employees just to answer the phones, and 1992 sales were nearly $2 billion. As Michael Dell says of his telephone sellers "They understand that everything starts with the customer."

Perhaps most flattering, competitors such as IBM and Digital Equipment are beginning their own phone and mail operations.

The $50 or so you pay for an AAA membership may be the best money you spend all year.

UP TO SPEED

Today a fax is as vital as a phone for salespeople. Your customers and your prospects almost all have fax machines. If you have one, you can send documents back and forth immediately: You can avoid the delay, expense and aggravation of using overnight delivery services.

A personal computer (PC) is also becoming a basic business tool. Depending upon your line of work, you may want to do some calculations on the computer. Even if you don't, you'll certainly find that a PC is a powerful vehicle for your correspondence, including prospecting letters.

If you have a PC, you can add a modem with a modest additional investment. With a modem, you can use an electronic bulletin board, also known as a bulletin board system, that runs automatically, 24 hours a day.

Suppose, for example, one of the insurance companies you represent brings out an annuity with a bonus yield for the first year. Instead of calling all of your clients or sending them letters, you can post an announcement on your electronic bulletin board. Wherever they are, your customers will get the message on their own PCs. If they want more information, they can answer by entering a message into their terminals. They can even buy directly, relying on the electronic bulletin board to take the order. You, or someone on your staff, can take whatever follow-up steps are necessary.

As more individuals and companies learn how to use electronic bulletin boards, they'll become an increasingly valuable resource for salespeople.

That's certainly not an exhaustive list. By the time you read this book, there may be new technological advances worth exploring. Always be alert to anything that can leverage your time and thus help you spend more of your day selling to more customers.

SUMMING UP

- To sell in the 1990s, you should make the most of the available technology.
- You want access to a phone, wherever you are, and you want your clients to be able to phone or fax you at any time.
- The purchase and operating costs of these devices will be modest if they increase your productivity.

If something makes you more productive or makes it easier for your customers to place orders, you should take advantage of it.

18

▼

When the Going
Gets Tough . . .

"The secret of success is constancy to purpose."

BENJAMIN DISRAELI

"If you don't drive your business, you will be driven out of business."

B.C. FORBES

Are we in a recession? Since 1989, economists have been arguing about it, each one pointing to his or her favorite statistic. Nonetheless, however you define recession, there's no doubt that the late 1980s and early 1990s have been difficult years in many sections of the United States. Jobs are down, and unemployment is up. How can you sell to people who barely have enough money to pay the rent, much less buy cars or mutual funds?

The answer is simply, Work at it. Work harder and work smarter. Keep your eye on your fundamentals and keep prospecting. If you're selling something that meets a genuine need, you'll sell it.

Even if the economy is down, with 8 or even 10 percent unemployment, that still means 90 or 92 percent of the people are working. You should *go where the money is*. If production workers are being laid off, salespeople can focus on teachers and other government employees. They're earning money and spending it; they're buying food and clothing and all sorts of other things.

There's always something that's hot. If people aren't buying big cars, they're buying compacts. If they're not buying big cars or compacts, they're buying light trucks. If you fish where the fish are, you'll get bites.

The real danger in a weak economy is the way it affects your attitude. *Often a recession is all in your mind.* Just like the hot-dog vendor who took down his sign because he heard business was bad, your sales will dry up if you "take down your sign." The problem is with you, not with the economy.

I've never had a recession. Throughout the late 1980s and early 1990s, my production has continued to increase. That's because I've never stopped. I've never let up. I've never taken a vacation. Even though I've become successful, with a huge client base, *I still run scared all the time.* I keep prospecting and adding new clients to that base.

▼▼▼

Always be alert to anything that can leverage your time; this will help you spend more of your day selling to more customers.

A salesperson is like an athlete. If you're off the tennis court for two or three weeks, you won't be razor-sharp. When football players lay off, they sometimes get timid and afraid to hit and be hit. That kills salespeople, too: They stop working, they get timid and they're afraid to get hit by rejections.

Football coach Ara Parseghian said that the fundamentals of the game are simple. You block, tackle and run, and you keep doing it; you don't get complacent. It's the same for salespeople. If you stick with the fundamentals, your game will hold up, and so will your sales, no matter what the economy is like.

RICHES IN NICHES

You think you're handicapped because of the product you sell? No one wants to buy it any more? Be thankful that you don't sell electronic organs. Since 1977, annual U.S. organ sales have declined from 222,400 to 13,300 in 1991, a decline of almost 95 percent.

What can you do in such a situation? Find the one customer group that really will buy this product, and push hard at that market.

When Robert Fletcher looked at the declining organ market, he also saw an expanding population over age 65. Seniors, he observed, tend to spend a lot of time in shopping malls. Many are lonely, so they're looking for company, for some way to spend their time in retirement. Malls offer safety and the companionship of other seniors.

Therefore, Fletcher established Fletcher Music Centers with one marketing purpose: to sell organs to people over age 65 in shopping-mall stores. He sells not only the organ but free lifetime lessons for the buyers and their families. Thus, these classes become social gatherings for retirees. Classes take hot-dog breaks while offering events such as Hawaiian Night.

When Japanese organ companies began bringing out high-tech organs to sell to younger people, how did Fletcher respond? He acquired the name of a defunct organ company, Estey, and conducted customer focus groups to discover what his target audience really wanted. In other words, he followed the basic rules of selling: *Ask questions, shut up and listen.*

If you're selling something that meets a genuine need, you'll sell it.

Fletcher learned that retirees didn't like all the little buttons and tiny letters on these organs. As a result, Estey organs (now manufactured in Italy) came out with a special line of organs with large lettering, to make them easier to read, and enlarged controls, to make it easier for arthritic fingers to operate them. All organs offer free lifetime service. Fletcher's motto is "Our customers must not be just happy—they must be delighted."

Has this philosophy paid off? Fletcher is singing a happy tune these days. While the industry declines, Fletcher Music Centers has become a $25 million business, growing at 25 percent annually. He now employs 200 people at 21 locations throughout Florida. Plans for national expansion are in the works.

THE PASSING LANE

Another troubled area is the mobile home industry: From 1984 through 1991, national mobile home shipments fell from 295,000 to 170,000. But that didn't stop Jim Clayton from putting the finishing touches on his rags-to-riches story.

When Clayton was growing up in Tennessee, his father picked cotton and his mother worked in a shirt factory. He got up at 5:00 A.M. to milk cows before going to school. "I dreaded holidays," Clayton recalled later. "Thanksgiving meant back-breaking farm work."

Clayton worked his way through college, buying and selling used cars through the classified ads. He sold a couple mobile homes that way and discovered that mobile home sales used the same financing, the same prospecting and closing techniques, and appealed to many of the same customers as the market for cars. Mobile homes also had higher profit margins.

So Clayton Homes was founded. Clayton insisted that homes be ready to show to customers only an hour after being unloaded from the manufacturer. He found that he could borrow to buy homes and sell them in a matter of days, often before the loan was due.

Thanks to this emphasis on moving quickly to meet people's needs, Jim Clayton waxed while his industry waned. From 1984 through 1991, Clayton Homes' earnings grew at a 23 percent compound annual rate, and the company's market share rose from 1.8 percent to 7.4 percent. Along the way, Jim Clayton, sharecropper's son, amassed a net worth of more than $250 million.

Go where the money is.

I THINK I CAN, I KNOW I CAN

If you have a desire to succeed, you will, no matter how depressing your circumstances. All it takes is an idea and the courage to carry it through. If you don't think this is true, imagine what it would have been like to be a young black man, homeless and sleeping in the parks of New York City in 1990, when the local economy was abysmal.

That was the situation facing Chris Jeffers. He slept in the park by day, when it was safer, and hunted for discarded beer and soda cans at night. On a typical night he'd find 600 to 700 cans, redeemable at 5 cents apiece, so he'd earn $30 to $35 a night.

Then he had his idea: He discovered that redeeming the cans wasn't easy. Many storekeepers didn't want the hassle of dealing with homeless people and their carts filled with cans. There were nonprofit centers to fill the gap, but they typically were open during the daytime; many nighttime can collectors needed cash right away for their drug and alcohol problems.

So Jeffers opened up a two-for-one service. He bought $40 worth of cans for $20, making a $20 profit when he cashed in the cans the next morning. With that profit, he bought more cans, and so on. Lured by service and convenience, homeless can collectors began to make the trip to Manhattan from Brooklyn and other parts of the city to sell their cans at half price. As one man said, "No hassle, no waiting, no sorting, just cash on delivery."

By 1992 Jeffers was working 16-hour days, handling over 100,000 cans a week in the good weather. Even after expenses (he owns a truck, rents an empty theater and employs three full timers and some part timers), he makes an estimated $60,000 to $70,000 a year. Instead of sleeping in the park, Jeffers lives in an apartment and has his own bank account. He has another dream, too: He wants to expand his operation nationally, as an expediter of recycling rules.

If Jeffers can prosper and strive for more, despite incredibly adverse circumstances, do you really have any excuse for not using the talent that God gave you?

Often a recession is all in your mind.

SUMMING UP

- No matter what the economy is like, you can sell.
- Selling in a recession takes hard work and a product that fills a genuine need.
- Go where the money is—sell to prospects who still have jobs and job security.

I still run scared all the time.

19

▼

Breaking with the Buddy System

"When the wine goes in, strange things come out."

JOHANN CHRISTOPH FRIEDRICH VON SCHILLER

Say "salesperson" to some people and the image of the infamous three-martini lunch is bound to arise. According to this view of the world, a salesperson's job is to take the buyer out to lunch, order drinks until judgment is lost and then produce a contract for a wobbly signature.

Obviously, nobody does business this way. Nevertheless, some salespeople still think lavish entertaining is part of their job. They think that if the client drinks, runs around and so on, that salespeople should, too. That's how they get business.

But that's not the case. Business entertainment is not necessary. I've never done any, and that's never hurt my sales. In fact, *people who overindulge in drink, drugs or sex don't like to do business with other people like that.* They don't trust salespeople who demonstrate those vices: Clients think a heavy-drinking salesperson will betray them by betraying their confidences. I've seen many sales blown because a salesman went after a client's wife or secretary. Even telling an off-color joke can offend some customers, so why take the chance?

KEEP YOUR DISTANCE

A lot of business entertainment takes place because the salesperson wants to be a buddy for the prospect. Many salespeople think that once you're friends, you'll get the business.

Again, that approach won't work. I never get close to my clients. Thus, I can be objective about them. If I become convinced they're taking the wrong path, I can put pressure on them to do the right thing. I don't have to worry about breaking up a friendship because there's no friendship between my clients and me.

Salespeople get killed when they stop working, get timid and become afraid to get hit by rejections.

SIGN 'EM, DON'T WINE 'EM AND DINE 'EM

As I've indicated, most business entertaining is unnecessary and even harmful to your sales career. Your customers should buy from you because you offer a valuable product or service, not because you take them to a play or a ball game or a weekend at a golf resort. If your clients start to think of you as a procurer rather than a professional, you'll never get their respect, and you'll never get the lion's share of their business.

That doesn't mean you should never do any business entertaining. You may want to take a good client out to lunch once in a while; breakfast or dinner may be a good time to meet with a prospect.

The key here is to keep the focus on business rather than on entertaining. When you take someone out for a meal, look for a quiet spot where you can really talk. Avoid the "in" places where tables are crowded together and the patrons spend more time table-hopping than they spend eating.

Drink only in moderation, if at all. Be sociable, but don't overdo it. Get your customer or prospect talking, and keep the conversation focused on something relevant to your business. That is, if you're selling office products, ask questions about your customer's job, but if you're selling life insurance, steer the conversation to his or her family, plans for retirement, business succession and so on.

In short, treat a meal with a customer like any other sales call, except it's one that takes place in a restaurant rather than in a home or an office. If you get the prospect talking, suggest an appropriate product and handle any objections, you can close the sale by the close of the meal.

EYES ON THE PRIZE

Although sales contests are not a form of business entertainment, they enjoy similar appeal among salespeople. Who doesn't like the idea of a free trip to Hawaii or Italy with their spouse (or significant other), where the company will treat you better than royalty?

If you stick with the fundamentals, your game will hold up, and so will your sales, no matter what the economy is like.

There's nothing wrong with winning sales contests, but they shouldn't spur you to greater efforts. *You should make a supreme effort all the time, with or without a sales contest. If you need a contest to turn you on, you really don't love what you do.*

I love every minute of my job, so I sell as if a contest is on every minute of every day. And that's paid off. If you push yourself all the time, you'll wind up earning enough to take those trips to wherever you want to go, even without a sales contest.

SUMMING UP

- It's not necessary to engage in lavish business entertainment. In fact, you can hurt yourself encouraging clients to engage in excess behavior because they won't trust you.
- If you become too close to your customers, you won't be able to give them objective, impersonal advice.

- A business meal can be a means of extending the working day, as long as you keep the focus on business.
- Winning a sales contest is fine, but you should devote full effort to selling all the time, whether or not a contest is under way.

Ask questions, shut up and listen.

20

▼

Taxing Matters

"Cursed war and racking tax
Have left us scarcely raiment to our backs."

SIR WALTER SCOTT

"There is one difference between a tax collector and a
taxidermist—the taxidermist leaves the hide."

MORTIMER CAPLIN, IRS COMMISSIONER

"I hold in my hand 1,379 pages of tax simplification."

CONGRESSMAN DELBERT LATTA

Success in selling is not an unmixed blessing. The more you sell, the more money you'll make, and the more taxes you'll owe.

At the same time, you become a bigger target. The IRS, naturally, goes where the money is. If you earn $200,000 a year, you're a lot more likely to be audited than someone who earns $20,000. The larger your income, the more the IRS hopes to collect by examining your return.

Does that mean you have to spend your life in fear of the big, bad IRS? Not at all. I get audited every year, yet I've never had any problems. There are a few simple things you can do to stay out of trouble, no matter how much tax simplification complicates the tax code.

First, keep good records. Write down every place you go, everything you do and every dollar you spend. This documentation will help your tax preparer compile your returns, and it will prove invaluable if you are audited.

Business entertainment is not necessary.

Second, have your taxes prepared by an expert. (A former IRS agent does mine.) If you do your own taxes, you're bound to make mistakes, and you'll probably draw the attention of the IRS. The same is true if you ask your cousin or neighbor to do your taxes for you. It's money well spent to hire a professional tax preparer who knows the ins and outs of dealing with the IRS.

Finally, don't hide income. Whatever you make, declare it. Nothing infuriates the IRS as much as unreported income. Other disputes (e.g., was a particular meal really a legitimate business expense?) can be resolved, but hiding income is a fast track to a new wardrobe of horizontal stripes.

TRAVEL A STRAIGHT AND NARROW PATH

Salespeople are particular targets for the IRS, and the area most likely to get scrutiny is travel and entertainment (T&E). That's where the IRS looks for abuses.

To substantiate your T&E deductions, you need to keep a log. Every time you engage in any type of entertaining, write down the details: whom you entertained, the nature of the relationship (e.g., a sales prospect), when and where the entertainment took place, the business purpose and the amount you spent.

Do this right away. If you use a credit card, write the details on the back of the charge slip. It takes only a few minutes. The sooner you write it down, the more accurate it will be and the more the IRS will believe you.

If you belong to a club that you use for business entertaining, you have to keep track of expenses there all year long. According to the tax law, you can't deduct any of the club dues unless you use the club more than 50 percent of the time on business.

So make sure that you meet the 50 percent threshold, even if you have to do more entertaining at your club at the end of the year. If you meet the test, you'll get a partial write-off; if your business use of the club falls below 50 percent, you won't be able to write off any of your dues.

People who overindulge in drink, drugs or sex don't trust salespeople who do, too.

MIXING IT UP

What about trips that are part business, part pleasure—sales meetings at resorts, for example? Your travel costs are deductible if the trip is primarily for business. In the eyes of the IRS, that means you spend more time at work than at play. So keep a complete log, hour by hour. And make sure the hours in the meeting room total up to more than the hours on the golf course.

For foreign travel, the rules are a bit stricter. Unless you're an employee taking a short trip (less than a week), you'll have to allocate time between business and pleasure and write off only the business portion. Again, you need to keep an extremely detailed log. Bring home a copy of any educational program you attend, along with your notes on the presentations.

Another red flag, as far as the IRS is concerned, is taking a T&E deduction for your spouse as well as for yourself. Sometimes these deductions are valid: you and your spouse go out to dinner with a client and spouse who come in from out of town. Generally, though, your spouse's deductions are legitimate only if he or she plays a real role in your business. Your best bet is to keep careful records, and then leave it up to your tax professional to determine what's deductible.

DRIVE TIME

Another contentious area for salespeople is the business use of your car. Again, the key is to keep a daily log, down to the mile, denoting whether each trip is for business or personal use. (You can purchase mileage logs at a business supply or stationery store.)

If you use your own car, you have two choices. First, you can add up all your business miles and multiply that total by an IRS standard allowance, which changes every year. Or you can find the exact amount you spent on your car during the year and deduct your percentage of business use. Typically, the latter technique results in the largest deduction, but you need thorough records to take advantage.

What if you use a company-provided car for selling? Once again, a mileage log is a must. Then, depending on the company's policy, you can reimburse it for personal use or pay taxes on the imputed income that results from your personal use.

Write down every place you go, everything you do and every dollar you spend.

HOME SWEET HOME

If you work at home, you probably would like to take a deduction for a home office. Then you can write off a portion of your electric bill, heating bill and so forth, as well as depreciation for part of your house.

There are two ways to qualify for a home office deduction. Either way, the office must be used regularly and exclusively for business. So don't put a television in there that the kids can watch when it's convenient.

If your home office is used regularly and exclusively for business, you're entitled to a deduction if it's your principal place of business.

That is, you have no office other than the one in your home. The other path to home office deductibility is to use the room to meet with clients and prospects.

KID STUFF

I've previously emphasized the need for salespeople to free themselves of mundane tasks so that they can devote more time to selling. I've suggested hiring teenagers, the elderly and the disabled to do various household and office-related tasks.

If you hire teenagers, there's no reason why you can't hire your own kids. Some or all of the money you pay can be deducted as a business expense. Of course, your kids will have taxable income, but they'll probably be in a lower tax bracket than yours. Thus, your family keeps more, and the IRS gets less. Moreover, your kids will learn what it means to work for money. They'll pick up work habits that will serve them well throughout their lives.

You can hire your own kids, but don't try to abuse the system. Pay them a fair wage for work they actually do. Again, good record keeping is essential. Of course, you wouldn't try to cheat in this area, would you? That's certainly not the lesson you want to teach your kids.

Have your taxes prepared by an expert.

SUMMING UP

- Higher-income individuals, especially salespeople, are vulnerable to IRS audits.
- The best protection is thorough record keeping. Keep a regular log of all your travels and expenses.
- If you keep a room in your house for business use and it's not used for anything else, you may be entitled to home office deductions.
- Hiring your children to handle household and office chores can make tax sense and contribute to their sense of responsibility.

▾▼▾

Hire your own kids, but don't abuse the system.

PART FOUR

▼▼▼

Conversations with Joe Gandolfo

You should make a supreme effort all the
time, with or without a sales contest.

▼▼▼

You can never remeet a person again for the first time.

21

▼

First Things First

"To listen is an effort, and just to hear is no merit. A duck hears also."

LET'S TALK ABOUT IT

Q: Joe, how would you advise a salesperson to get started?

A: There are two things I'd say to every salesperson, including rookies and veterans.

Q: What's first?

A: You can never remeet a person again for the first time.

Q: In other words, you get only one chance to make a good first impression.

A: Right. And a positive first impression will help you sell, while a negative first impression is hard to overcome.

Q: What's the second thing all salespeople should know?

A: God gave you two ears and one mouth, so He meant for you to do twice as much listening as talking. No one ever learns anything by talking.

▼▼▼

God gave you two ears and
one mouth, so He meant
for you to do twice as
much listening as talking.

CLEAN BODY, CLEAN MIND

Q: Let's start with a good first impression. Does that mean you should always look your best?

A: Well, a salesperson should always be well groomed—hair trimmed, nails clean and so on. You should dress conservatively, unless you're in an industry where you're expected to be stylish. That means dark colors—blues, grays and browns. Don't be flamboyant. But there's more than your clothes to a good first impression.

Q: How you present yourself?

A: It's not what you say as much as the nonverbal cues. You need to watch your body language and your facial expressions. More sales are lost because of how you act or look than through high prices or lack of product knowledge.

Q: Can you give an example?

A: Suppose I walk up to a prospect and say, "Hi, I'm Joe Gandolfo," but I don't like his shirt or his tie, so I wrinkle up my face. I haven't said anything, but he can see in my face that I don't care for the way he dresses, so he won't buy anything. Or if I walk into your office and see a stupid-looking swordfish on the wall and I make an expression of disgust, you're not going to buy anything from me.

Q: Keep your disgust in check.

A: Or suppose I walk into your home and the first thing I look at is your good-looking wife or daughter. I won't sell you anything because my eyes are telling you what I find really important.

Q: A male prospect won't like your roving eyes.

A: It's not just that you're looking at his wife or daughter. Say we are having breakfast or lunch. This attractive woman walks by, and I start talking to her. You won't buy anything from me.

▼▼▼

More sales are lost because of how you act or look than through high prices or lack of product knowledge.

Q: Why not?

A: Because you're saying to yourself, "I am very busy, and I am the most important man here. You should look at me and listen to me.

Because you're not, I'm not buying what you're selling, even if you're giving it away, because you're not interested in what I'm saying."

EYES RIGHT

Q: What's the lesson here?

A: Whenever you speak to someone, don't you like it when he or she looks at you? The same is true with clients.

Q: Look them right in the eye.

A: That connotes sincerity and trustworthiness. But you can't look someone in the eye unless you're right with the Man Upstairs. If you've got something on your mind, you can't look someone in the eye.

Q: You can tell?

A: Sometimes I look people in the eye, and as soon as they look down, I know that they're not right with themselves, and I don't want to have anything to do with them. The same thing happens to you when you're selling. If you can't look into a client's eye, you won't make a sale. You don't lose sales for technical reasons.

Q: So you look people in the eye?

A: Not just when I'm selling. When my kids would say, "Hey, Daddy," I would put everything down, whether or not I thought anything they had to say was significant. Because they were speaking, it was important to them, so I listened.

▼▼▼

You can't look someone in the eye unless you're right with the Man Upstairs.

ALL EARS

Q: What do you do when people don't listen?

A: One time at a restaurant, I blew up at a waiter. Before I had come to town, I had made a special stop for sourdough bread. I asked to have it toasted, but it came back sliced and buttered. He wasn't listening to me. Telephone operators, too, frequently don't listen, and I get annoyed when I have to repeat myself. I'll stop someone in the middle of a conversation if they're not listening to me.

Q: Aren't you overreacting a bit?

A: Not really. Most people feel that way, even if they don't express it as I do. You can bet that your prospects like you to listen to them.

Q: So, if a client talks, you should listen.

A: I follow two rules, and my staff does, too. *First, whenever you talk to human beings, look in their eyes.* And second, *whenever you listen to human beings, look at their eyes or their mouth.*

Q: And that will help you sell?

A: Those are signs of genuine sincerity. They will do more for your sales than any technical information ever will. *Selling is 98 percent understanding human beings and 2 percent product knowledge.*

Q: Besides looking at the right part of a prospect's face, shouldn't you pay attention to what the client is actually saying?

A: You should. When a client talks, no matter what he or she is saying, the words that come out really mean, "Dummy, pay attention; then I'll tell you how to sell to me."

▼▼▼

Whenever you talk to human beings, look in their eyes. Whenever you listen to human beings, look at their eyes or their mouth.

CRASHING THE GATEKEEPER

Q: That's a good strategy after you meet face-to-face with a prospect. But how do you get in to see prospects?

A: When I first started, I used two approaches: (1) the phone and (2) personal contact. Basically, they were both the same.

Q: What were they?

A: I'd say, "I don't want to sell you anything now, but I would like an opportunity to meet with you sometime next week to share an idea that's been a help to other accountants (or auto dealers or journalism

▼▼▼

Selling is 98 percent understanding human beings and 2 percent product knowledge.

professors) here in Cincinnati (or Lexington or San Antonio). If the idea fits your philosophy and pocketbook, fine. If not, I'll go away."

Q: Why did you approach them this way?

A: First of all, most salespeople want to sell to people right away. They come in and say, "Put everything aside." They don't know what kind of family or business crisis the prospect is facing. Salespeople should respect their prospects. Put yourself in their shoes.

Q: That's why you don't demand an appointment right away?

A: Instead, I indicate that I want to make an appointment for the next week. That approach says "I know you're busy, and I appreciate that." At the same time, it indicates that I'm busy, too, so I want to schedule an appointment a week from now. Then the prospect thinks, "This guy's different from all those other clowns who just want to sell me something."

Q: Okay, so that's why you ask for an appointment in advance. Why do you say that you want to "share an idea"?

A: For one thing, the prospect is bound to be more interested in sharing an idea than in buying something. Who doesn't want to share an idea?

Q: And for another thing?

A: When you come down to it, *the only things people have to sell are ideas, and that's all people are interested in buying.* You buy a wash-and-wear shirt because you don't want to have to iron it. You buy a television with a remote control because you want to be able to change channels while you're lying on the couch. When my son reached driving age, he wanted mag wheels and a sunroof; I don't think he even cared if a car was attached. People buy the idea, not the thing.

When a client talks, no matter what he or she is saying, the words that come out really mean, "Dummy, pay attention; then I'll tell you how to sell me."

Q: That's true in life insurance, too?

A: Sure. One prospect said to me, "I bought from this agent because he told me that if I become disabled, his company will pay all the premiums." I didn't even think of saying that; I took it for granted that all prospects knew that. But the other agent was smart. Instead of saying, "Every insurance company will pay premiums if you become disabled," he said, "We'll pay the premiums if you become disabled." The client bought the idea.

Q: Are all life insurance ideas so grim?

A: One approach I use is to ask the question "Do you want to pay Uncle Sam, or do you want to pay yourself?" That's an idea a lot of people find appealing. The ideas between your ears are the only things that make you different from any other salesperson. People buy you, not the company you represent.

SUMMING UP

- First impressions are crucial.
- Salespeople should do twice as much listening as talking.
- When clients speak, look at their eyes or mouth.
- Don't show disinterest or disrespect, verbally or nonverbally.
- When you're prospecting, ask for a future appointment rather than assuming that the client will see you right away.
- Tell the prospect that you'd like to "share an idea," which is really what you're selling, regardless of your product line.

"I'd like an opportunity to meet with you next week and share an idea. If it fits in with your philosophy and pocketbook, fine. If not, I'll be on my way."

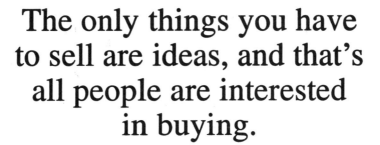

The only things you have
to sell are ideas, and that's
all people are interested
in buying.

22

▼

Special Forces

"Do not shorten the morning by getting up late; look upon it as the quintessence of life, as to a certain extent sacred."

ARTHUR SCHOPENHAUER

Q: All right. You've explained why you ask for an appointment next week, to "share an idea." How about the part where you bring in "all the other accountants in Cincinnati" or whatever?

A: Everybody, no matter what their occupation, thinks that their problems are unique. They're really not—it's just a game people play. But they all want to deal with a specialist, so I play along. I even say "an idea that's been a help to other neurosurgeons," rather than "other doctors," because neurosurgeons think their problems are different from those of obstetricians or gynecologists.

Q: Calling yourself a specialist helps your credibility?

A: When you go in for open-heart surgery, do you want a surgeon who does the operation once a month or one who does it every day? When my wife Carol had some cosmetic surgery on her leg, she went to the Mayo Clinic, where she found a doctor who's been doing that procedure seven times a day, every day, for 28 years. He knows more about that surgery than some guy who does it four times a year. That's why she went there.

▾▼▾

Everybody, no matter what their occupation, thinks their problems are unique.

Q: Why do you throw in that part about Cincinnati or Lexington?

A: Everybody likes dealing with someone who knows the local area. Why buy insurance from a guy with an office a thousand miles away?

EARLY TO RISE

Q: After you get their agreement to share an idea with you, what do you say?

A: I ask the question, "Would next Thursday at 7:00 A.M. be convenient, or would 7:30 be better?"

Q: Joe, do you really do business at 7:00 A.M.?

A: Definitely. I make 90 percent of my sales before 9:00 A.M.

Q: Prospects wake up in the morning with an irresistible urge to buy life insurance?

A: That's not exactly how it works. There's a saying that "people who are successful want to do business with people who are successful." That's a bunch of garbage.

Q: What's the truth?

A: In reality, *people who get up early and go to bed late like to do business with other people who get up early and go to bed late.* The prospect knows the salesperson has paid the same price for success.

Q: Successful people are early risers?

A: John Paul Getty's advice was "Rise early, work hard, strike oil." The people who are the most successful are the busiest people, so they need to be up early. If a salesperson wants to sell to me, he or she better be there at 6:00 A.M.

Q: Do you really find someone to call on that early?

A: In my younger days, I'd get up early and drive an hour or more to meet with Florida ranchers and farmers. Many of them said, "You're the only one who ever showed up at 6:00 A.M. to do business, and that's why I'm buying from you."

▼▼▼

I make 90 percent of my sales before 9:00 A.M.

Q: Do you think that's unique to Florida?

A: If you say, "You can't do that in my area of the country," you haven't been up at that time, and you don't know who's up. I guarantee you, the best doctors and lawyers in your area pay a dear price. That's the reason they got there and are still there. They got to be the best through long hours and hard work, so they're bound to be up early.

Q: And if you're up then and selling, you'll get their business.

A: The first large case I ever sold goes back to my early days in Lakeland. I was at mass, at 6:30 A.M., when a 68-year-old lady came up to me and said, "Young man, I've been watching you. I found out you're in the insurance business. My lawyer says I need a $1 million policy. Will you sell it to me?"

Q: Sounds like an offer you couldn't refuse.

A: It was a $68,000 commission. Now, I wasn't at mass, praying for a 68-year-old lady to come along and buy a $1 million policy, but the fact that I was up and around at that hour helped me get the business.

IN WITH THE "UP" CROWD

Q: Was that the only big sale you landed just by being up early?

A: No. When I first came to Lakeland, I rented this tiny office. I parked the car in the lot there about 5:30 every morning. One morning I found a card on my windshield. It was the card of a lawyer in my office building, and it said, "Meet me in my office."

Q: What did you think?

A: I was scared to death. I thought I might be in his parking spot.

Q: So what happened?

A: I went to see him, and he said, "Young man, I've been watching you for three or four months. You're the only person in this town who's ever beat me to my office. I want you to write life insurance on each member of this firm."

▼▼▼

People who get up early and go to bed late like to do business with other people who get up early and go to bed late.

Q: That was really lucrative?

A: It was just the start. He also introduced me to his breakfast club, which met every morning at 6:00 A.M. at the local pancake house. They were pillars of the community, wealthy people who needed large amounts of life insurance, and I sold to every one of them. Had I not been up, I'd never have met those people.

Q: Any other advantages to getting up early?

A: When I was younger, older people would say to me, "You remind me of myself when I was a young man, so I want to do business with you."

Q: Can you relate to that now?

A: Sure. Whatever I need to buy, I only see salespeople at 6:00 A.M., on Fridays. If they come, I buy because they remind me of me.

Q: Any other thoughts on getting up early?

A: When it's appropriate, I'll say, "Can I meet you at 6:30 A.M.? I've seen your car by your office then." And the prospect will think or even say, "Really? You must be an early riser, too." I can't say this enough: People who are up early like doing business with people who are up early.

Q: That's been a big advantage versus other salespeople?

A: If I had asked for an appointment at nine or ten o'clock in the morning, I'd have run into all sorts of excuses. At six or seven o'clock, people don't have any good reason not to see you.

YOUR TIME IS MY TIME

Q: What if a prospect doesn't want to talk about buying life insurance at 7:00 A.M.?

A: Then I fit the customer in whenever he or she wants. Each customer is thinking, "From eight to five o'clock, I'm making money. I don't want to take time out from making money to talk about something that will make you money." So I meet early, I meet late and I meet when customers break for lunch. Sometimes I have three breakfasts or three lunches in one day. I tell my customers that I'm on call 24 hours a day: "When you're not making money, give me a call so we can talk."

Q: You fit your schedule to suit your clients?

A: Successful people are busy. Their attitude is, "Tell me everything I need to know in the shortest period of time, so I can make a decision."

▼▼▼

At 6:00 or 7:00 A.M., people don't have any good reason not to see you.

Q: What if you just can't start selling before dawn?

A: If you want to sleep late, you can work until midnight. Take what fits into your own personality. The important thing is to work as long and as hard as you have to. As George Allen said, "Leisure time is that five or six hours when you sleep at night."

Q: The rest of the time you pursue your goals.

A: I agree with these words of George Bernard Shaw: "People are always blaming their circumstances for what they are. I don't believe in circumstances. The people who get on in this world are the people who get up and look for the circumstances they want, and if they can't find them, make them."

Q: For salespeople, the words "get up and look for the circumstances" really mean "get up and look for the prospects."

A: The numbers game works. When I first started, I might call 150 people to get 20 appointments. At that time, I might sell insurance to one out of seven prospects. I made up in effort for what I lacked in finesse.

Q: Now you're longer on finesse and shorter on brute energy?

A: Now I have more knowledge of people. I understand human nature better. In my early presentations, I stuck to the script: Switch the pen at this word; pound the table over here. Once you truly understand human beings, your batting average goes way up.

SUMMING UP

- You can help your credibility by indicating that you're a specialist in the buyer's business.
- You're more likely to sell to successful people early in the morning.
- The more prospecting you do, the more you'll sell.

Each customer is thinking, "From eight to five o'clock, I'm making money. I don't want to take time out from making money to talk about something that will make you money."

23

Friendly Persuasion

"After the verb 'To Love,' 'To Help' is the most beautiful verb in the world!"

BARONESS BERTHA VON SUTTNER

Q: Joe, so far we've covered the methods you used when you first started out. What do you do now that's different?

A: Rather than make cold calls on total strangers, I prospect with referred leads.

I say, "I need your help." When you ask for help, no one ever says no.

Q: How do you get the referrals?

A: From other prospects and clients.

Q: How do you manage that?

A: I owe it all to a drunken paint salesman.

Q: Sounds like a good story.

A: After I had been selling for a few years, I called upon a guy living in an apartment who obviously had been having a spirited evening.

Inside, I saw plaques and trophies all over. Here's the conversation we had:

> JG: What are these plaques and trophies for?
>
> Drunken Paint Salesman (DPS): I won them for being the top paint salesman in the United States.
>
> JG: How did you become number one?
>
> DPS: Because I know the magic words.
>
> JG: What magic words?
>
> DPS: I say, "I need your help." When you ask for help, no one ever says no.
>
> JG: What help do you ask for?
>
> DPS: I ask for the names of three friends.

Q: And those three friends are the referred leads?

A: Right. You'll notice that he didn't ask for "some names," or five or ten names. He asked for three, which is a number most people are comfortable with. Psychologists and psychiatrists say that people think in threes. Besides, there aren't many people with more than three good friends.

Q: What do you do after you get the names of three friends?

A: I try to find out how old they are, how much money they make and so on. Then, before I leave, I say, "Will you see them before next week? If so, would you mind mentioning my name? And would you mind if I mention your name? I'll approach them on the same professional basis I've approached you."

THE BUDDY SYSTEM

Q: Then what?

A: My paint salesman had some more advice. Suppose John Jones referred me to Sam Smith. I'd call Sam Smith and say, "Has John Jones mentioned my name to you?"

Q: So that became your opening line?

A: Right. Whether or not John Jones had mentioned my name to Sam Smith, it's a great way to start a conversation. Remember, you get only one chance to meet someone for the first time.

Q: And after your opening line, you can ask if the prospect wants to share an idea and make an appointment for next week.

On selling to friends: You grab them around the neck, hug them and say, "Is there any reason we can't do business?"

A: That's right. "If the idea fits your philosophy and pocketbook, fine. If not, I'll go away." It's all the same, except you're working with referred leads. Going through the prospect's mind is that you were recommended by his or her closest friend. The prospect thinks, "If this guy's good enough for him, he's good enough for me. The least I can do is show him the courtesy of listening to him." You get many more appointments that way.

Q: Did your drunken paint salesman have any other magic words?

A: He told me how to approach close friends.

Q: How do you do that?

A: You grab them around the neck, hug them and say, "Is there any reason we can't do business?"

A PATENTED APPROACH

Q: Joe, how do you handle people who won't give you an appointment?

A: I get the same excuses as anyone else: "I have enough insurance," "I don't like life insurance," etc.

Q: What do you say to them?

A: I use my "patent office" strategy.

Q: What's that?

A: First, while they're objecting, I shut up and nod, as if I agree with what they're saying. Then, before I leave or hang up, I say, "May I ask you a question?" The prospects are at ease, and they figure they've about finished with me, so they tell me to ask my question.

Q: Which is . . . ?

A: I sort of lead up to my question by relating that in President John Adams's administration, early in the nineteenth century, the federal government came within three votes of abolishing the patent office. They thought they had already invented everything that could be invented, so what was the point of having a patent office?

Q: The government thought we had reached the limits of technology?

▼▼▼

"Have you closed your patent office?"

A: That's right. This was before telephones, automobiles, light bulbs, airplanes or televisions. Even later, in the middle of a technological explosion in 1899, Charles H. Duell, commissioner of the U.S. Office of Patents, urged President William McKinley to abolish the patent office. Duell said to McKinley, "Everything that can be invented has been invented."

Q: So, after you tell them this bit of history, what question do you ask?

A: I ask, "Have you closed your patent office?"

Q: Meaning, "Have you closed your mind to new ideas?"

A: Exactly. If you had a store, wouldn't you want the latest merchandise on the shelves? No matter what business you're in, you probably go to seminars to upgrade your performance level. Well, there are new ideas and concepts in life insurance, too. The tax laws change almost every year. I say to the prospect, "I have new ideas, and all I want to do is run them past you. If they fit your philosophy and pocketbook, fine. If not, I'll be on my way. Now, do you have any objection?"

Q: Does that approach work?

A: Sometimes, but not always. Some people just have closed minds.

Q: Okay. One way or another, you get a lot of appointments, and they're a week away. Then what?

A: My secretary calls to confirm the appointments. It looks professional and keeps me from wasting my time on broken appointments.

CREDIBILITY COURSE

Q: How do you handle the sales call, after you actually get there?

A: After I go in, I always seat the prospect on my right. All I have with me is a yellow legal pad.

Q: Then what?

A: First, I put my business card on the table in front of me. I say, "There are thousands of life insurance agents and financial advisers, so I think you should know what my qualifications are. You can see from my business card that I'm a life member of the Million Dollar Round Table. That's an industry award—only a few thousand people in the entire industry are life members."

Q: You're establishing your credentials.

A: Right. Then I go on to point out the NQA on my card, explaining that NQA means that over 90 percent of the people I have done business with are still doing business with me. That indicates that I like long and enduring relationships, so I will stay in close contact with all prospects, reviewing their programs.

▼▼▼

Once they trust me and my ability, they are ready to buy from me.

Q: What else have you managed to get on your card?

A: After my name is the designation CLU. That stands for *chartered life underwriter*, which is comparable to a CPA in the accounting field. I also say that I'm a member of the Catholic church and that I give numerous talks throughout the United States on life insurance.

Q: Not every salesperson is going to have such a resumé on a business card. What can salespeople do if they're just starting out in sales?

A: When I was younger, I used to say to customers, "I'm on schedule for the Million Dollar Round Table" or "I'm on schedule to become a CLU," etc. Whatever your accomplishments are, state them. There's another plus to this approach.

Q: What's that?

A: If you have any pride and you keep saying you're "on schedule" for this or that, you'll accomplish it.

Q: What's the point of starting a sales call with advertisements for yourself?

A: This way I eliminate uncertainty. My prospects have been saying, "I don't know you, so I don't trust you." As a first step, they must know what qualifies me to talk about this subject. Once they trust me and my ability, they're ready to buy from me.

SUMMING UP

- Prospecting with referred leads is much easier than making cold calls.
- To get referred leads, ask other customers and prospects for help.
- If prospects won't see you, ask if they've closed their minds to new ideas.
- If prospects will see you, begin the sales call with a summary of your own credentials so your prospects can get to know you, trust you and buy from you.

24

▼

If You Don't Probe,
You'll Get the Shaft

"I keep six honest serving-men
(They taught me all I knew)
Their names are What and Why and When
And How and Where and Who."

RUDYARD KIPLING

Q: Joe, you've explained why you start out each sales call by establishing your own credibility. What's the next step?

A: I say, "I want to ask you some questions."

Q: Don't all salespeople do this?

A: Not at all. When I request permission to ask questions, the prospect thinks, "This is the first guy to ask me what I want." *People buy what they want, not what I want,* so I want to find out what they want.

Q: That seems like a reasonable approach.

A: It may be reasonable, but it's usually overlooked. The biggest breakdown among salespeople is the tendency to push a certain product down everyone's throat *this week*—whatever the manager says to move. No matter whether the prospects are single, married, rich, poor, no matter how many kids they have, it makes no difference—sell them this month's special.

PRESCRIPTION FOR DISASTER

Q: These salespeople may be wasting their time selling something that's neither needed nor wanted.

A: What if doctors said, "All salespeople must take this prescription" without any examination? Half would probably die. Well, that's what salespeople do.

Q: They have something to sell, so they sell it.

A: Exactly. A salesperson might say, "I've got a piece of real estate I'd like to sell to you." If the prospect asks why, the salesperson says, "I just thought you'd like to buy it." But why would the prospect want real estate—for tax shelter, for income, for appreciation? That's what the salesperson should have asked me in the first place.

▼▼▼

People buy what they want, not what you want.

Q: Find out what the prospect wants before you try to sell anything.

A: It's a great way to break down the personal barriers. It's comparable to being in a bar or at a dance and meeting an attractive person of the opposite sex. You tell each other about yourselves, and after five minutes, you say, "Gee, honey, I feel like I've known you all my life."

Q: Not only do you want to know prospects; you want them to feel like they know you.

A: That's what you're trying to do. Then prospects will think, "I know you, I like you, I trust you. Now I'll listen to what you have to say."

Q: What kinds of questions do you ask your prospects?

A: I might say, "I'd like to ask you what you think about life insurance and investments." I ask about insurance on the spouse, on the kids and about college plans. I ask if they prefer permanent life insurance or term insurance. I don't care what they say, I jot it down. If they say that they're going to give their kids back to the orphanage, I just write it down.

Q: What kind of answers do you get?

A: I often get some revealing information. If you don't ask questions, you can go through your whole presentation and get to the end, where you're ready to sign the application, and the client says something like "It doesn't make any difference if I'm a cropduster, does it?"

Q: Not exactly a great risk for the insurance company.

A: Or the client says, "I'm having open-heart surgery next week."

PATH OF LEAST RESISTANCE

Q: So listening can steer you away from wasting your time on presentations where the insurance company won't approve the application. How can listening help you make sales?

A: I can't begin to tell you how many times I've come in after another agent who has tried to sell the prospect permanent insurance.

Q: That's life insurance with a savings component. The client pays high premiums, and the agent collects high commissions.

A: So I'd say the following:

JG: What do *you* want?
Prospect: Term insurance.
JG: I think you need term insurance.

▼▼▼

The biggest breakdown among salespeople is the tendency to push a certain product down everyone's throat this week.

The prospect thinks I'm a genius.

Q: Term insurance is "pure" life insurance, with lower premiums and lower commissions.

A: Sure, I get higher commissions on permanent insurance. But I figure I'll sell term now because that's what the client wants. *Next year, after the client loves me, I'll come back and sell him or her permanent term* if that's what he or she really needs. You shouldn't try to change a person's philosophy, at least not at first.

Q: Do other salespeople sell what they're supposed to sell, not what the client wants to buy?

A: Most salespeople get annoyed with their clients:

> Client: I believe in term insurance.
> Typical salesperson: What's wrong with you? Don't you know permanent life is better?
> Client: Wait a minute. You asked me what I thought; you didn't ask what I thought *you* thought.

Q: Is this common in other industries?

A: Sure. For example, you go into a store, and the salesperson says, "I want to show you this gray suit." Maybe you didn't come in to buy a suit; you just want a tie. Or you go into a dealership, and the salesperson says, "Let me show you this car," when all you wanted were some hubcaps.

Q: The car salesperson could use your approach instead.

A: Of course.

> Car salesperson (CS): Can I help you?
> Buyer (B): I want to buy a car.
> CS: What kind did you have in mind?
> B: A Camaro.
> CS: What color?
> B: Red.
> CS: Two or four doors?
> B: Four.
> CS: How about your budget?
> B: I can't afford more than $400 a month.
> CS: Fine. I'm going to sell you what you want.

▼▼▼

The prospect will think, "I know you, I like you, I trust you. Now I'll listen to what you have to say."

Q: Getting back to life insurance, what if the prospect doesn't know the difference between term and permanent life?

A: If they say, "Joe, I have no idea about insurance, and that's why I asked you to come," then you have permission to make suggestions.

Q: What do you do?

A: I say, "May I make a suggestion?" No one says no to that. Then I can recommend whatever, in my opinion, best suits their needs.

Q: How do you arrive at your recommendation?

A: I ask all kinds of questions—how old are you, how old are your kids, how much are you able to save and so on. I write down all the answers on legal pads.

Q: Can you get sales tips this way?

A: During this type of conversation, prospects often say something like "I've been reading about this deferred annuity," for example. Then I pull up my seat and say, "That's the idea I want to share with you." They think I'm brilliant. And they buy. You sell them what they wanted to buy all along. Later you can sell them what they need.

Q: It's easier the second time around?

A: Yes, because the prospect says, "Because you were so smart the first time, you can come back any time."

▼▼▼

Next year, after the client loves me, I'll come back and sell him or her permanent term.

SUMMING UP

- Before trying to sell anything, question prospects to find out what they need or want.
- Most salespeople go the other way and try to push whatever they're told to sell.
- Sell clients what they want. After they know and trust you, you can come back and sell them what they really need.

▼▼▼

"May I make
a suggestion?"

25

▼

Same Time, Next Year

"After ecstasy, the laundry."

Q: After you make a sale, do you do anything to reinforce the client's decision?

A: I always write a thank-you letter. Here's the form:

Dear Pat:

Tonight does not seem too soon to congratulate you on this afternoon's decision about your new life insurance policy. This is certainly a major step in establishing a sound future financial program. I hope that our meeting was the beginning of a long and enduring relationship. Thank you again for your business, and I wish you every success possible.

Sincerely,

Joe Gandolfo

Q: Do you have any special process for recognizing important clients?

A: I send a plaque with this saying to everyone who buys a $1 million policy from me: "Many people look at things and say why; I dream of things that never were and say, why not?"

Q: What do your clients think about these plaques?

A: Lately, I've been specializing in sales to auto dealers. I often speak at their meetings. At these meetings, I hear them ask each other, "Do you have a plaque?" It's like a little club. Everybody wants to belong.

Q: In effect, they're saying, "My life is worth a million dollars. Is yours?"

A: A lot of my clients display their plaques in their home or office. They say to me, "That's the nicest thing anyone has ever done for me." It's a means for me to tell clients that I appreciate their business. That's why I have 94 percent persistency.

Q: What else do you do?

A: I send my clients birthday cards and Christmas cards. I can't begin to tell you how many additional policies, on children and spouses, I've sold because of those cards. Young salespeople should do this kind of thing, just like your manager told you. It works, especially if you keep it up for five years or more.

▼▼▼

You sell prospects what they wanted to buy all along.

Q: What other kind of follow-up do you do?

A: I deliver the first policy a client buys and go over it with him or her. Then I say, "I'll make you two promises."

Q: What are they?

A: I say, "I'll see you once a year to go over your program. And I'll keep you up to date on tax changes, etc., that might affect your program."

Q: What do you ask them to do in return?

A: I say, "I want two promises from you. First, I want you to allow me in your home once a year to review your program. Second, whenever you're called upon by another insurance salesperson, give that person my card and say that I do all your buying for you."

Q: So each side makes two promises.

A: I say, "I'll keep my promises; will you keep yours?"

EXIT LINES

Q: If you go through your entire presentation and the client won't buy, what do you do?

A: In that case, I say, "I'd like to ask two questions before I leave." Most people agree.

Q: And those two questions?

A: First, "What financial formula did you use to arrive at the amount of life insurance you have?" Then, "Who's reviewing your program every year like all the other intelligent auto dealers or neurosurgeons in Cincinnati or Lexington?"

Q: What does this accomplish?

A: It makes the client stop and think, "Why do I have this much insurance? Why isn't anyone reviewing my program? I'm intelligent, aren't I?"

Q: And they buy?

A: Sometimes. Sometimes it's just hopeless. All you can do is give it your best shot.

BEGINNERS' PLUCK

Q: What advice do you have for salespeople starting out today?

A: See people who are around your age and income. They'll have problems you can understand.

Q: Why do you say that?

A: When I was young, I tried to do estate planning.

You'll grow with your clients.

Q: You tried to sell life insurance to help older, wealthy people offset what they'd lose in estate taxes.

A: I tried, but I failed miserably. I just didn't understand the clients' problems. Similarly, single people don't understand married people's problems.

Q: You had a hard time selling to wealthy people back then?

A: Yes. The clients would be thinking, "What does he know about my problems?" Now I understand their problems, so I'm comfortable with them, and clients realize this.

WHERE THE MONEY IS

Q: Is estate planning a major area of your business now?

A: Definitely. I sell a lot of sizable policies for estate planning purposes. The reason I can sell them now is that I'm older, I make more money and I understand the problems faced by wealthier people, who buy the large policies.

Q: Your clients realize that you do pretty well?

A: Today millionaires listen to me because everyone I call on knows I make more money than they make. That's why they listen—I know their problems.

Q: How do you approach them now?

A: The first thing I do is ask about the estate plan. You'd be surprised how poor most plans are. Over 98 percent of wills I review, for example, have no guardianship clause for minor children if both parents die.

Q: What else do you look for?

A: If the prospect owns a small business, I ask if a buy-sell agreement is in place and if it's funded with life insurance. I also ask about a stock redemption plan, mortgage insurance on the building and key-man insurance on the company he or she just acquired. Is the prospect taking advantage of retirement plans? I ask all the questions, not taking anything for granted.

Q: What about clients who aren't business owners?

A: If the client has a large estate, I ask if a gifting program is under way. Don't automatically assume that everything already is taken care of, just because a client is wealthy. I find that 85 percent of all lawyers and CPAs don't know the law in my area. Whatever your area, other "experts" may not be expert.

"Would it affect your standard of living?"

Q: So you say, "Your lawyers and CPA screwed up"?

A: Hardly. I'm not out to pick a fight with my client's professional advisers. Instead, I say, "I'd like several hours of your time one afternoon, with your CPA and attorney there as well." Then we all get together, and I let the professionals do my selling for me, telling the client what he or she ought to do. If everyone is there, a decision can be made.

Q: How do you approach the attorney and the CPA?

A: I say, "I'm a consultant, a catalyst to get your client to do what you've been trying to get [him or her] to do. I may make recommendations, but you make the decisions."

Q: Aren't a lot of insurance salespeople, young and old, tempted to go after that big-ticket business?

A: Many try, often at the urging of their general agents. But general agents make a mistake when they tell young salespeople to go into estate planning. *If you don't understand clients' problems, they won't listen to you.*

SUMMING UP

- After you make a sale, send thank-you letters to assure your prospects that they have put their trust in the right person.
- You may want to devise special ways of saying thank you to key customers.
- Sending birthday and Christmas cards to your clients can be an inexpensive way to gain follow-up sales.
- Promise your clients that you'll see them at least once a year, to keep them up to date, in return for their pledge to be loyal customers.

- If prospects won't buy, ask if they really have the expert advice that they need.
- Salespeople should concentrate on people approximately their own age and income. That way, they'll be able to understand their customers' problems.

"You can either pay more or buy less. Which would best fit your present financial situation?"

26

▼

Growing Gains

*"It is always growing weather. Only the ignorant and the
blind believe that the soil ever comes to rest."*

PIERRE VAN PAASSEN

Q: You've advised young salespeople not to call on older, wealthier
clients. When do they get to move up in class?

A: If you start young, you'll grow with your clients. When you're
30, deal with 30-year-olds. When you're 40, deal with 40-year-olds,
and so on.

Q: So where can a beginner start out?

A: Pick an area you understand, perhaps IRAs. If it's a product a
young, not-too-rich client might reasonably buy, a young, not-too-rich
salesperson can identify with this client.

Q: What if the client says he or she can't afford to buy?

A: You can ask the client the following questions:

JG: Are you saving any money?
Client: Some.
JG: If you took the money you're saving and put it into an IRA,
would it affect your standard of living? Would it take the food off
your table or force you to skip a vacation?
Client: Well, no.

JG: All right. Just let me give you an idea. If it doesn't fit your philosophy and your pocketbook, I'll be on my way.

Q: Then what do you tell your client?

A: I point out my product's advantages. If it's a savings vehicle I'm trying to sell, I'll tell the client that banks can't guarantee his or her money as long as an insurance company can and that banks don't have an annuity that can pay out for the rest of his or her life.

Q: Any other tips?

A: I'll often say, "That's why all the other auto dealers (or doctors, etc.) in town are putting their money into insurance companies and not in banks." Remember, everyone thinks their industry has unique financial concerns.

"Your premium can only go higher."

ILL OMENS

Q: Are there some special problems you have to handle in your industry?

A: Rated cases can be a challenge.

Q: These are clients with health problems or high-risk occupations, so they have to pay higher-than-standard premiums. What do you do?

A: Suppose I told the client he or she could buy a $100,000 policy for $2,000 a year in premiums. After the physical exam, the client gets a lower health rating, so the $100,000 policy will now cost $2,400 a year. I'll then have two policies issued: (1) a $100,000 policy with a $2,400 premium and (2) perhaps an $87,500 policy with a $2,000 premium.

Q: Then what?

A: I'll tell the client the following: "There's something wrong with your body. You can either pay more or buy less. The company may readjust your rating after a year or two. In the meantime, which would best fit your present financial situation?"

Q: Which do most clients choose?

A: That depends. I remember one client from early in my career. He was a 30-year-old lawyer who was having a relationship with a married woman. The company found out and charged an extra $400 premium.

Q: Did the company fear that a jealous husband would shoot him?

A: I was scared to tell him. I said the underwriter, the insurance company, offered to take the rating off—that is, reduce the price—if he ended his relationship. He got very angry at first but then decided, "Well, she's worth $400 a year."

Q: So he paid the extra money?

A: Two years later he wrecked a car, with the woman in it. He was drunk, and they were both killed. Thus, those underwriting departments know what they're doing.

THE SALE THAT NEVER ENDS

Q: Can you sell life insurance to people who really don't need insurance—those with no dependents?

A: With such people, I say, "There are three things that determine what you pay for insurance: your age, your health and your occupation. Each year you wait, rates go up 3 percent, just because of your age, and you don't know what will happen to your health. Your premium can only go higher."

▼▼▼

"Buy some for tomorrow, while it's on sale."

Q: You tell clients to buy now because they might need some later?

A: If a client is single, she might need only a small policy for burial costs. But if she projects out ten years, she may be married with kids and a mortgaged home. Then she'll need to educate those kids. So why not buy now, when you're young and healthy? Yes, I sell life insurance to single men and women. I say, "Buy some for tomorrow, while it's on sale."

Q: Does this buy-on-sale strategy only work for young single people?

A: I do the same thing with older clients. Suppose a client has a buy-sell agreement in place for his business. If he dies, his partner will need $400,000 to buy him out, and vice versa. Well, next year, if the business grows in value, the buy-sell might be for $550,000. Five years from now, it might be $1 million. So why not buy a $1 million policy now, at age 54, rather than waiting till age 59, when the rates will be much higher?

OBEY THE LAW OF AVERAGES

Q: What other advice do you have for young salespeople?

A: When you start, try to meet tons of people and get millions of responses. Don't overlook prospects. *You never know who's going to make it big.*

Q: The more prospecting you do, the more likely you are to strike gold.

A: You don't need to be bright to know that if you work from 5:00 A.M. to 10:00 P.M., seven days a week, you'll come across more people than you will if you work 8:00 A.M. to 5:00 P.M., five days a week. The more exposure you get, the more you can sell.

Q: Can you sell to night owls, as well as early risers?

A: A lot of people work late—night auditors, night-shift operators, workers, hospital lab technicians and so forth.

Q: And you'd go after all of them.

A: I'd say "Would you have any objection to reviewing your life insurance with me" (or whatever product you're selling) to every human being you possibly can meet.

You never know who's going to make it big.

Q: Even those with no visible means of support?

A: Everybody. I ask what will happen if they die or become disabled. That establishes the need for life insurance. Then I ask what will happen if they retire and live a long life, which leads me to a discussion of permanent life insurance and long-term cash values. Then I say, "Which best fits your present financial situation?" Even if they start out paying only $25 a month, I get them to fill out the forms. That starts them off; they become my clients.

Q: From there, you hope for bigger things.

A: Some of your clients will grow, and you'll grow with them. Young lawyers, accountants, etc., leave their firms and start their own firms. Employees become employers. You ride their coattails.

Q: What if they don't want you to come with them?

A: The only reason you lose their business is that you don't grow with them and don't see them each and every year. The greatest liability of youth is impatience. Everybody has to pay dues.

PICKING UP SPEED

Q: Do you have an example of how you grew with a client?

A: I sold a policy to a fellow who was 19 years old and about to become a father. He bought a $5,000 term policy, with a premium of $24 a year.

Q: Presumably, that increased.

A: A year later, he moved to Daytona Beach and went into business with his father-in-law, who owned Daytona Speedway and was the largest auto parts manufacturer in the United States for racing cars. The father-in-law had a heart attack, and the young man moved up in the organization. Now he has a $7.2 million policy on his life, with an annual premium of $168,000, plus a pension and profit-sharing plan.

The only reason you lose your clients' business is that you don't grow with them.

Q: Quite an increase.

A: Another client of mine inherited money. Now he's in prison somewhere, not buying a lot of insurance. You never know who's going to make it.

Q: So you sink your teeth into your clients early and never let go.

A: My secretary calls every client to arrange annual meetings. I keep up with them all.

SUMMING UP

- Young salespeople can start with young clients and grow with them.
- If clients say they can't afford to buy, ask if buying will affect their life-style.
- You can often sell your product now, when the need is low, because the price will increase in the future, when the need is greater.
- Prospect as widely as you can. You never know who is going to make it big.

▼▼▼

"Many people look at things and say why; I dream of things that never were and say, why not?"

27

▼

Last Words

That's all you need to know to sell and grow rich. Make sure your fundamentals are in order and implement my sales techniques. You don't have to follow them slavishly, but apply those that fit your personality and your business.

I'll close with the words I use when I address a large audience: It's most unfortunate I won't get to know you all personally, but I hope, through these words, we have met.

"I'll see you once a year to go over your program. And I'll keep you up to date on any changes that might affect you."

▼

Afterword

"There is only one success—to be able to spend your life in your own way."

CHRISTOPHER MORLEY

THEY SOLD AND GREW RICH

Some salespeople go through life working for one employer and wind up doing very well. Other salespeople, however, go into business for themselves as independent reps selling for several companies. Still other people go from one form of selling or another to running and operating their own business.

If you're in business for yourself, you'll certainly have more responsibilities and headaches. But the payoff may be greater—in psychic terms as well as cash income.

After you have your fundamentals in order, you can think about becoming an entrepreneur or an independent contractor. Here are some success stories for the 1990s—from people with modest incomes to multimillionaires.

HAT TRICK

When I was discussing first impressions, I said that salespeople should dress conservatively rather than flamboyantly. That's true in most lines of business and in most industries. However, there are times when you want to draw attention to yourself and stand out from the crowd.

Put yourself in the shoes of Heida Thurlow, who, in January 1979, was selling at a housewares trade show at Chicago's McCormick Place. Thurlow was a 39-year-old, divorced mother of two who was far from her homeland, the German island of Sylt.

She needed money but was unable to get a job in her profession, which was mechanical engineering. Thus, she was trying to start up a cookware import business. However, she was tucked away in a tiny booth at the back of the exhibit hall and had virtually no orders coming in.

"What financial formula did you use to arrive at the amount of life insurance you have?"

What did she do? She went shopping. She spent $35 on a 1940s-style, wide-brimmed black hat. The hat caught the attention of a top executive with a major mail-order catalog. He liked Heida's style and, upon inspection, liked her roasting pans, too. The roasting pans went into his catalog, and she had her start on what has become a $10 million business. Now she owns 100 such hats, which have become her trademark at shows and other industry meetings.

Of course, Heida Thurlow didn't become a $10 million woman because she wore spectacular hats. She had her eye on what her customers wanted, right from the beginning. For example, she started out importing German enamel-on-steel pots, but she didn't like the lids: She thought they'd be too heavy for U.S. women. Also, she knew her customers would prefer to see through the lids while cooking. So she substituted lighter glass lids from Japan. Similarly, she designed stainless steel handles for the lids with an air pocket that would stay cool so her customers could take the lids off while the pots were on the stove.

Besides a fashion sense and ingenuity, Heida Thurlow has courage. Struck by cancer, she fought the disease through chemotherapy and radiation treatments and battled the cancer into remission.

HORSE SENSE

Another dress-for-success story belongs to John Peterman, a former salesman who lost his job in the 1980s and found himself with a wife, four kids and a $10,000 American Express debt—not mention a mortgage that was two months overdue. Peterman went to work as a consultant, specializing in the food industry.

During his travels, Peterman found himself in Jackson Hole, Wyoming, where he bought a horseman's duster, which is an ankle-length canvas coat. Soon almost everyone he met was asking where he got the coat.

So Peterman contacted the manufacturer and began ordering coats for resale. Within a few years, the business had expanded into a catalog of unique items, *Booty, Spoils & Plunder*, grossing $2 million a year. As Peterman says, "Success is the process of not accepting failure."

MISFORTUNE INTO FORTUNE

What looks like a disaster can sometimes be turned into an advantage. Imagine how James Winner, Jr., felt on that night in 1985 when he walked out into a parking lot and discovered his car had been stolen. Instead of giving in to despair, Winner saw an opportunity. How many other people, he wondered, were similarly victimized each year? Wasn't there a need here, a need he could address?

"Who's reviewing your program every year like all the other intelligent . . . in town?"

Therefore, in 1987, he launched Winner International Corporation, which distributes an automotive antitheft device he created, called

"The Club." In 1991, his company made $60 million selling Clubs in the United States. Expanding sales to Europe, Australia and even China, Winner International's 1992 goal was $120 million. A real winner! Moreover, Winner International provides full-time employment for 80 people at its Sharon, Pennsylvania, headquarters.

Before starting his own company, Winner was a marketing manager, so he thinks like a salesperson. Now that he has a distribution organization in place to sell The Club, why not sell other products? That's what he's doing with Animal Lover, a device that attaches to a car ignition and emits an ultrasonic sound that alerts animals up to 50 yards ahead that a vehicle is coming.

Three of Winner's four children help manage his company. They, like all employees, find inspiration in the sign that dominates Winner's office: "Focused efforts transform visions to realities."

DON'T SELL YOURSELF SHORT

A lot of salespeople complain that they can't sell because their product is priced too high. The competition, of course, has a low-priced model. Squeezed by financial concerns, the buyer purchases the cheaper brand. That's why sales are lost.

Don't you believe it. If customers bought on price alone, everyone would drive a Chevrolet or a Volkswagen; no one would have a Cadillac or a Mercedes. Hotels would all be Days Inns or Holiday Inns, while Hyatt and Marriott would be out of business.

Obviously, that's not the case. People buy an idea, not a price. If you have the idea they want, they'll pay for it, even if you charge a higher price. In fact, you may be selling your product at too low a price, not too high a price. When customers really want something, they may pay more than you expect.

See people around your age and around your income.

Every salesperson should remember the story of Andronico Luksic, the son of a Croatian migrant worker who came to Chile. Back in 1954, when Andronico was 26, he acquired the rights to a copper mine in northern Chile. However, he didn't have the resources to develop the mine on his own, so he offered to sell the rights to Japan's Nippon Steel. His asking price was 500,000 Chilean pesos, then worth $45,000 (U.S.). Nippon Steel accepted. In fact, the Japanese thought that the offer was in U.S. dollars, not pesos, so they sent him a check for $500,000! This story demonstrates that when you have something a customer really wants, you'll be surprised how much he or she will pay for it.

With that beginning, Luksic expanded the family fortune to over $1 billion, and the Luksic Group became Chile's first true multinational corporation. His motto is "Follow the philosophy of the ant." If you focus on accomplishing the little things, you'll wind up moving mountains.

THAT'S NOT CHICKEN FEED

Listening to customers and watching them has paid off in a big way for Johnnie Bryan Hunt, who started as poor as anyone can conceive. He grew up in Arkansas during the depression, dropped out of school after the seventh grade and worked in his uncle's sawmill for $1.50 a day. As a teenager, he would sell the mill's leftover wood shavings to help support his six brothers and sisters. Who would buy wood shavings? Poultry farmers who needed chicken coop litter.

After a stint in the army, Hunt bought a livestock barn that went under. To pay off his debt, he drove a truck seven days a week, earning $40 a week selling cement and sod to make a little extra money.

While driving a truck, he noticed that some of the farmers on his route burned rice hulls. Rice hulls, he thought, would make good litter for chicken coops, so Hunt started his second business. When the chicken litter business turned downward, Hunt painted a horse on the package, increased the price 50 cents and sold horse litter to breeders.

Hunt eventually gained the confidence of one of his customers, the manager of a Ralston Purina facility. That manager was having trouble with the trucking company that hauled dressed chickens; he suggested that Hunt buy the company. So Hunt went into his third business.

▼▼▼

If you don't understand your clients' problems, they won't listen to you.

Bucking the industry trend, Hunt relied on company-owned trucks that were driven by well-groomed employees in clean uniforms. This impressed Hunt's customers, including the late Sam Walton and other employers in the region. Hunt eventually became the first big trucker to cooperate with railroads and signed a deal with the Santa Fe Railway to offer door-to-door, truck-and-rail customer service between California and the Midwest. To keep up with his changing market, he often accompanies salespeople on calls.

By 1992, Hunt's net worth climbed to $375 million. Reportedly, he has been grooming his son Bryan to take over the company. "Bryan has a lot to learn," Hunt said. "Mostly, how to listen."

Index

KEEP YOUR COMPETITIVE EDGE WITH MORE BESTSELLERS FROM

REAL ESTATE EDUCATION COMPANY

Also available at your local bookstore.

	ORDER NUMBER	PRICE	QUANTITY	TOTAL AMOUNT
1. **Buyer Agency, 2nd Edition,** by Gail Lyons and Don Harlan	1978-03	$24.95		
2. **Classified Secrets: Writing Real Estate Ads that Work, 2nd Ed.,** by William H. Pivar and Bradley A. Pivar	1926-01	$29.95		
3. **Fast Start in Property Management**, by Karl Breckenridge	5608-50	$19.95		
4. **How About a Career in Real Estate?**, by Carla Cross	1907-08	$14.95		
5. **How to Profit in Commercial Real Estate Investing**, by John B. Allen	4105-09	$34.95		
6. **The Landlord's Handbook: A Complete Guide to Managing Small Residential Properties**, by Daniel Goodwin and Richard Rusdorf, CPM	4105-08	$21.95		
7. **Multiply Your Success with Real Estate Assistants**, by Monica Reynolds	5608-89	$79.95		
8. **New Home Marketing**, by Dave Stone	1909-03	$39.95		
9. **New Home Sales,** by Dave Stone	1909-01	$34.95		
10. **New Home Selling Strategies,** by Nancy Davenport-Ennis	1909-06	$24.95		
11. **Power Real Estate Advertising,** by William H. Pivar and Bradley A. Pivar	1907-05	$24.95		
12. **Power Real Estate Letters: A Professional's Resource for Success**, by William H. Pivar and Corinne E. Pivar	1926-03	$29.95		
13. Book with 3-1/2" IBM-compatible disk	1926-09	$79.95		
14. Book with 5-1/4" IBM-compatible disk	1926-10	$79.95		
15. **Power Real Estate Listing, 2nd Ed.,** by William H. Pivar	1907-01	$18.95		
16. **Power Real Estate Negotiation**, by William H. Pivar and Richard W. Post	1907-04	$19.95		
17. **Power Real Estate Selling, 2nd Ed.,** by William H. Pivar	1907-02	$18.95		
18. **The Property Manager's Handbook,** by Steven G. Pappas	4105-10	$32.95		
19. **The Real Estate Agent's Action Guide to Listing and Sales Success,** by Bob Deutsch	1908-07	$22.95		
20. **The Real Estate Investor's Tax Guide,** by Vernon Hoven	5608-71	$24.95		
21. **Real Estate Prospecting: Strategies for Farming Your Markets**, by Joyce L. Caughman	1913-07	$24.95		
22. **Real Estate Sales Survival Kit,** by Doug Malouf and William H. Pivar	1913-13	$24.95		
23. **Real Estate Wealthbuilding,** by Howard A. Zuckerman	5608-53	$24.95		
24. **Simplified Classifieds,** by William H. Pivar and Bradley A. Pivar	1926-02	$29.95		
25. **SOLD! The Professional's Guide to Real Estate Auctions**, by Stephen J. Martin and Thomas E. Battle, III	1903-31	$32.95		
26. **Staying on Top in Real Estate**, by Karl Breckenridge	1927-04	$18.95		
27. **Time Out: Time Management Strategies for the Real Estate Professional**, by John Ravage	2703-11	$19.95		
28. **Winning in Commercial Real Estate Sales: An Action Plan for Success**, by Thomas Arthur Smith	1909-04	$24.95		

Subtotal _____

Plus applicable sales tax and shipping charges _____

Total _____

Place your order today: By FAX: 1-312-836-1021. Or call toll-free 1-800-437-9002, ext. 650. In Illinois call 312-836-4400, ext. 650. Or fill out and mail this order form. Please mention code R93004.

Real Estate Education Company / 520 N. Dearborn St. / Chicago, IL 60610-4354

☐ Payment Enclosed

Charge to: ☐ VISA ☐ MasterCard

Account No. _____

Exp. Date _____

Signature _____
(All charge orders must be signed.)

Name _____

Company _____

Street Address _____

City _____ State ____ ZIP _____

Daytime Phone (___) _____
(In case we have a question on your order.)

Return Address:

_____

_____

_____

Place
Stamp
Here

**Real Estate
Education Company**
a division of Dearborn Financial Publishing, Inc.
Order Department
520 North Dearborn Street
Chicago, Illinois 60610-4354

IMPORTANT—PLEASE FOLD OVER—PLEASE TAPE BEFORE MAILING

NOTE: This page, when folded over and taped, becomes an envelope, which has been approved by the United States Postal Service. It is provided for your convenience.

IMPORTANT—PLEASE FOLD OVER—PLEASE TAPE BEFORE MAILING

262-903 - 3905